eXpressDSP™
FOR
DUMMIES®

by Steve Blonstein
and Maher Katorgi

WILEY

Wiley Publishing, Inc.

eXpressDSP™ For Dummies®

Published by
Wiley Publishing, Inc.
111 River St.
Hoboken, NJ 07030

www.wiley.com

Copyright © 2004 by Wiley Publishing, Inc., Indianapolis, Indiana

Published by Wiley Publishing, Inc., Indianapolis, Indiana

Published simultaneously in Canada

For general information on our other products and services or to obtain technical support, please contact our Customer Care Department within the U.S. at 800-762-2974, outside the U.S. at 317-572-3993, or fax 317-572-4002.

Wiley also publishes its books in a variety of electronic formats. Some content that appears in print may not be available in electronic books.

ISBN: 0-7645-2488-7

Manufactured in the United States of America

10 9 8 7 6 5 4 3 2

1O/TQ/QR/QU

WILEY   is a trademark of Wiley Publishing, Inc.

About the Authors

Steve Blonstein: Steve Blonstein is a technical director at Texas Instruments — Software Development Systems. He has spent the last 20 years involved in embedded systems, programming everything from the lowliest 8 bit microcontrollers to state-of-the-art 32 bit DSPs. He has spent the last 5 years at Texas Instruments focusing on the development of eXpressDSP — a programming methodology specifically designed for Texas Instruments' TMS320 family of DSPs.

When not trying to make it easier to program TI DSPs, Steve likes to spend time flying his plane and spending time with his wife, Andrea, and three children, Samantha, Danielle, and Nicholas, in their home in Palo Alto, California.

Maher Katorgi: Maher Katorgi is a member of the technical staff at Texas Instruments (TI) where he has spent the last three years helping drive and support TI's eXpressDSP software foundation technologies, including XDAIS, BIOS, and Reference Frameworks for TI DSP customers. He has over 14 years of embedded software design and development experience for biomedical, automotive, telematics, and audio-video applications. Maher holds an M.Sc. degree in Computer Engineering from Case Western Reserve University in Cleveland, Ohio.

When away from work, Maher likes to sharpen up his woodworking skills and spend time with his wife, Nisrine, and two daughters, Suma and Ranla.

Publisher's Acknowledgments

We're proud of this book; please send us your comments through our online registration form located at www.dummies.com/register/.

Some of the people who helped bring this book to market include the following:

Acquisitions, Editorial, and Media Development

Project Editor: Clark Scheffy

Technical Editor: Alan Campbell, Ron Birkett

Editorial Manager: Stephanie Corby

Permissions Editor: Laura Moss

Cartoons: Rich Tennant (www.the5thwave.com)

Production

Project Coordinator: Jay Kern

Layout and Graphics: Jill Piscitelli

Special Art: Rashell Smith

Proofreaders: Julie Trippetti

Indexer: Sharon Helgenberg

Special Help: Zoë Wykes

Publishing and Editorial for Technology Dummies

Richard Swadley, Vice President and Executive Group Publisher

Andy Cummings, Vice President and Publisher

Mary C. Corder, Editorial Director

Publishing for Consumer Dummies

Diane Graves Steele, Vice President and Publisher

Joyce Pepple, Acquisitions Director

Composition Services

Gerry Fahey, Vice President of Production Services

Debbie Stailey, Director of Composition Services

Table of Contents

Introduction

*T*oday, Digital Signal Processors or DSPs are everywhere. Chances are you've either knowingly or unknowingly used one in the last hour. DSPs have become the core of almost all digital cell phones, broadband modems, digital still cameras, MP3 players, and on and on. The beauty of the DSPs that power all of these devices is that they're programmable. About the only limitation is the creativity of the individual who is programming the DSP.

However, DSP development tools and DSP software have historically been behind the tools and software found on more general-purpose microprocessors. This lag has given DSP development tools and software the reputation of being difficult and cumbersome to program. In addition, it's no secret that much of the software running on a DSP is math intensive. In fact, we often hear programmers say that they're scared away by all the math.

Well, times change and in 1999, Texas Instruments (TI) led the charge to make DSP programming accessible to all through the introduction of eXpressDSP. eXpressDSP has eliminated much of the low-level programming needed to get the DSP up on its feet. In addition, it has created a vibrant market for ready-to-use (with that math intensity hidden) algorithms that enable a whole new class of applications. *eXpressDSP For Dummies* shows you how it's all done and enables you to quickly develop your own applications from the building blocks we provide.

Who Should Read This Book

Anyone considering using a DSP to power a product can benefit from reading this book. Software programmers can benefit from both the eXpressDSP overview information and the specific real-application example that we lead you through. For anyone dubious about the ease with which DSP can now be programmed, this book is a must read. And for you managers out there, watch out. This eXpressDSP stuff is going to make your engineers so much more productive that they'll be on the beach a lot more. Just wait until the marketing folks find out!

How To Use This Book

eXpressDSP For Dummies is organized in such a way that you can either read it like a novel from front to back, or use it as a reference book and simply refer to the Index to find the juicy part that you need. If you're completely new to this stuff, then we recommend that you become familiar with the concepts before operating the machinery. Think of a chainsaw: Impressive, but very dangerous in the hands of an untrained person.

How This Book Is Organized

This book is organized into three logical parts, all of which will enhance your knowledge and hands-on experience with eXpressDSP.

Part 1: Programming Principles in eXpressDSP

This part provides a useful overview of programming a DSP and goes into the specifics of how eXpressDSP helps solve many of the common challenges faced by the DSP programmer.

Chapter 1 covers the issues that make programming a DSP different from programming a general-purpose microprocessor. Getting things scheduled on a DSP is a particular challenge. Chapter 2 covers a unique software kernel that really takes care of the job. TI calls this kernel *DSP/BIOS*. As we mentioned before, math-intensive algorithms make a good part of a finished DSP software system. As more and more of these algorithms become available off-the-shelf, it's become increasingly important to get all algorithms to play by the same set of rules — think of cars on the road here. Having everyone agree to drive on the same side of the road really helps! Chapter 3 covers XDAIS, the element of eXpressDSP that addresses the "rules of the road" issue. Finally, Chapter 4 covers eXpressDSP Reference Frameworks. These are the shells of semi-custom DSP applications that leverage DSP/BIOS and XDAIS and bring it all together.

Part II: Building a Real Application Today

Part II leads you through the steps to put together a real working system. In this example, you will build a digital audio recorder/player. This system is like a simplified version of those portable digital music players you see all those teenagers using. OK, you've got one too — we won't tell.

Part III: The Part of Tens

A standard feature of all *For Dummies* books, each Part of Tens chapter provides ten useful bits of information for your consumption. Chapter 8 provides the ten top eXpressDSP resources. Chapter 9 lists ten amazing things about eXpressDSP that you won't find listed anywhere else.

Icons Used in This Book

We use several icons in this book to mark specific information. Here's what each icon means:

 This icon points out information that isn't crucial to understanding the book, but that you may find interesting if you like to know what's going on "inside the black box."

 A Warning icon points out information that you *definitely* want to read. Not doing so may expose you to a pitfall that is otherwise easily avoided.

 Tip icons are fairly self-explanatory — they set off tips such as shortcuts and ways to make your life easier.

 This icon marks information that should be stored away in the back of your mind — useful stuff that's good to fall back on as you continue to use eXpressDSP.

eXpress Assumptions and Other Important Stuff

eXpressDSP For Dummies focuses on the software that runs on the DSP itself — often referred to as the run-time software.

Another significant part of the eXpressDSP story is the development tools that you use to write, test, and deploy your DSP run-time software. These tools include the development environment (Code Composer Studio), DSP emulators, DSP simulators, and additional tools. This book doesn't attempt to lead you through the use of these tools and assumes that you use other available sources to find out about them.

We assume that you have access to one of our common DSP Starter Kits (DSK), like the TMS320C6713DSK. You may even have *eXpressDSP For Dummies* because it was included in the box of one these DSP starter kits, so you're obviously in good shape. These kits include the hardware and software for building and testing new DSP applications. If you don't yet have a DSK, they're available for purchase at a low cost. Check out www.dspvillage.com for more information.

Finally, the example application in Part II needs to be downloaded from the Web. You need a Web-enabled PC in order to get access to this code. To hear the application running, you need a music source like a CD player and some speakers or headphones. Don't worry, the teenagers have plenty of these.

The address for the companion Web site to this book is www.ti.com/dummiesbook. This Web site is where you can find software for making Part II of the book come together, as well as links to other DSP resources and products.

Where to Go Next

You may choose to try to build your first application based on the example in Chapter 7. Or you may want to leverage the principle concepts and build your own DSP application from the components that are readily available from Texas Instruments or TI's third party partners. Whatever your choice, hopefully your creativity is the only thing keeping you from your next product, and not the low-level DSP code or the math.

Part I
Programming Principles in eXpressDSP

The 5th Wave   By Rich Tennant

"We're here to clean the code."

In this part . . .

This part introduces you to the special capabilities of a Digital Signal Processor (DSP) and some of the challenges that arise when trying to program one. The four chapters in this part provide a high-level introduction to the eXpressDSP technologies: DSP/BIOS, XDAIS, and Reference Frameworks. The following chapters also provide a good insight to some of the basic techniques that Texas Instruments recommends to get the most from your time and the DSP you have chosen to use.

Chapter 1

DSPs — The Indy Cars of the Programming Road

Close your eyes and try to conjure up the following vision. Think of the typical family car. Sure, it gets you from point A to point B safely and is particularly good at stopping and starting at all those stoplights, yield signs, and annoying speed bumps that show up everywhere, but it doesn't give you the white-knuckle experience that a fine-tuned racing machine can deliver.

The microprocessor that powers your desktop or laptop PC is a lot like the typical family car — it does its duty, but for the most part, it doesn't get too exciting unless you really like spreadsheets.

Now put on your racing helmet and slither into an Indy Car at the Indianapolis Motor Speedway. When those infamous lights change from red to green, you slam the accelerator to the floor and you don't let up until the end of the race — you've just envisioned a DSP.

Four Unique Properties of DSP

DSPs are literally the Indy Cars of the Programming Road. They're fast and specialized and can deliver an experience to the user that goes way beyond suburban transportation.

In the following four sections, we give you the lowdown on the unique characteristics that make programming DSPs different from those "family car" microprocessors.

Super mathematician

First and foremost is math — DSPs are excellent at doing math. This feat is usually achieved with one or more arithmetic-logic units and one or more discrete multipliers. These units are designed to be extremely fast and to achieve their complete mathematical operation in a single cycle of the clock.

The real key to success is keeping the math units busy all of the time. Remember, Indy cars are designed for constant high speeds — they just don't start and stop well.

Just because the DSP is good at doing math doesn't mean that *you* have to be good at it (though it's great if you are). In this book, we show you how to acquire all kinds of cool algorithms to run on your DSP without ever having to get into the science and math involved.

Precious memories

The key to DSP programming success is its clever and efficient use of the limited on-chip memory. To put things in perspective, most modern low-cost DSPs have anywhere from 8 Kbytes to 256 Kbytes of internal memory. That's *Kilobytes,* not Megabytes. Cost and power-consumption issues control the memory limitation. (We cover power consumption in the "Power alert" section.)

The DSP programmer must be continuously thinking about how to make the best use of this precious internal memory. Sloppy programming in this area will have a dramatic negative impact on the overall DSP performance. In Part II of this book, we show you various tricks for managing this challenge.

Streaming data

DSPs do really well in applications where the data to be processed is arriving in a continuous flow, often referred to as a *stream*. The key is getting the data into the DSP, processed, and back off the DSP as efficiently as possible.

All kinds of fancy peripherals on the DSP help make this possible. Things like Direct Memory Access (DMA) controllers and Multi-Channel Buffered Serial Ports (McBSP) are just two of the types of peripherals useful in moving data around. The goal is to program these controllers to minimize CPU overhead so that the DSP can do its job and not have to worry about what the peripherals are doing. This also serves to keep that precious internal memory carefully filled with useful data for those magic math units to crunch on.

Power alert

Have you looked inside your PC recently? You can't actually see the microprocessor because it's buried under a fan. Current microprocessors consume anywhere from 10 to 100 Watts and need a lot of cooling to avoid turning to goo. That's OK when the power source is your National Electrical System.

Now imagine running that microprocessor on a single rechargeable Lithium Metal Hydride AA battery with a capacity of 1200mAh. Expected total lifetime of the battery will be about 11 minutes if the power required is 10W and just 1 minute at 100W.

Now consider the latest DSP systems that consume a measly 100mW while running flat out, pedal to the metal — under these conditions, the AA battery will last 18 hours. The challenge for designers is to programmatically make use of all of the power-saving techniques provided by the DSP.

Figure 1-1 shows the block diagram for a state-of-the-art DSP from the TMS320C55x DSP platform. These devices are some of the stingiest available when it comes to minimizing power consumption. Much of this is achieved by keeping just what is needed turned on at any particular time.

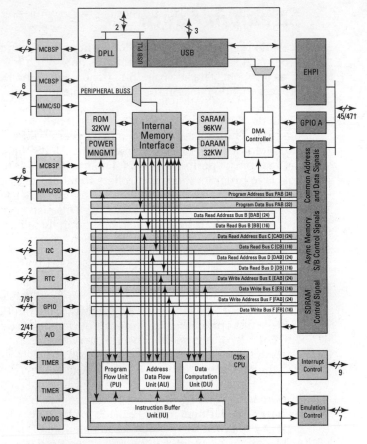

Figure 1-1: Block diagram of TMS320C5509 DSP.

Real real-time

The term *real-time* is one of those highly overused and abused terms. You probably got some real-time stock quotes this morning. (Better keep that daytime job for a while longer.) Was that really real-time? What is real-time? Is really fast really real-time? To clear up the confusion, we'd like to take a crack at defining what *we* mean by real time.

Consider the example of a system being used to compress a stream of speech data for passage through a communication channel. At the decoder end of the system, compressed data arrives in a continuous stream.

Now assume that a DSP is decoding this compressed stream. The DSP absolutely must keep up with the incoming compressed data as it arrives. This is *real* real-time processing. Failure to maintain real-time will result in some kind of dropped data and a pop or noise in the output that will annoy the decoder user. So, even if the decoder is really *fast,* it still may not be *real* real-time.

The technical side of DSP scheduling

The reality of modern day DSP designs is that the DSP is running several algorithms in some kind of time-sliced or pre-emptive scheduling environment. In situations like this, simply adding up MIPs doesn't guarantee success. For example, let's say that the DSP offers 100 MIPs of raw performance, and you need to run two algorithms simultaneously. Algorithm A consumes the entire CPU for 1.2mS every 3mS. Algorithm B consumes the entire CPU for 1mS every 2mS. In theory, it looks like Algorithm A will consume 40 MIPs and Algorithm B will consume 50 MIPs. That seems like a total of 90 MIPs leaving a comfortable margin of 10 MIPs. But wait, this is supposed to be a *real* real-time system, with each algorithm meeting a hard time deadline in order for the system to function correctly. In this case, whatever you try to do with the scheduling algorithm A and B, you will not be able to get real real-time despite the apparent "spare" 10 MIPs.

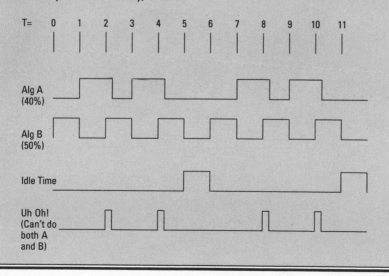

DSPs are often used in real real-time systems because if programmed appropriately, they're handily up to the task. Most general-purpose processors cannot be practically used in these situations.

DSPs Everywhere

Hopefully, we've convinced you that DSPs are fast, specialized, and responsive machines. That doesn't mean that DSPs are only useful in niche applications like medical instrumentation, military systems, and industrial control . . . nothing could be further from the truth.

DSPs are literally everywhere. Take a look at some of the product examples shown in Figure 1-2. These consumer devices are all manufactured in very high volume and are nearly ubiquitous in today's world. The widespread use and popularity of these devices is made possible because the DSPs are physically small, have a low cost, and have low power consumption (envision that single AA battery lasting 11 lousy minutes with one of those power-hungry microprocessors). On top of all that, they're really good at crunching numbers — there's plenty of that needed in the world of digital media.

Nokia 3650 phone

Kodak DX3600 digial camera

e.Digital Odyssey 1000 MPS player

Figure 1-2: Products that use TMS320 DSPs.

Chapter 2

Keeping a Schedule: The DSP/BIOS Kernel

Consider the following scenario: You are married with three children. (Some of you are already there — others of you are probably thinking this is a nightmare scenario!) The first major issue here is that the children outnumber the adults. Oh, and by the way, your million-dollar Silicon Valley condo only has one bathroom!

Now, consider a typical weekday morning. How do you manage getting everyone ready in about an hour from the time you all wake up to the time you all have to leave for school and work? Chances are you'll use some kind of schedule to share the precious resource (in this case, your condo's single bathroom). And, if you're really crafty, you may even figure ways to have multiple bathroom users at the same time, like one person in the shower while someone else is shaving.

Modern day DSPs juggle similarly limited resources and tasks. As we discuss in Chapter 1, a DSP includes several precious resources. These resources are typically the internal memory, the CPU itself, and limited physical DMA channels. The real challenge is to schedule these resources for the various competing functions on the DSP. Thankfully, these factions are more easily trained than the average two-year old.

Taking Advantage of a Scalable Software Kernel

Historically, DSP system designers would design their own homegrown schedulers. These schedulers were often simple round robin or hardware interrupt driven schemes. The problem with homegrown schedulers is portability, scalability, and maintainability. Typically, if the person who built the schedule left for greener pastures, your DSP scheduler quickly became a mystery.

Instrumentation for debug is also always a challenge. Just how many printfs can you put into a real real-time system and still expect the system to work?

The DSP/BIOS kernel addresses these challenges for the TMS320 DSP family, and it achieves this feat using a stingy amount of system memory and CPU cycles. We show you some more details later in this chapter.

Portability

The problem with homegrown kernels is maintaining portability. If you can predict the future, then you may be able to skip this section. However, portability is a big issue if you can't predict the future and don't know the details of the devices coming down your production line over the next several years.

DSP/BIOS offers a set of well-documented and robust APIs (Application Programming Interface — the interface through which the application calls and uses the individual BIOS modules) for each of its modules. The DSP/BIOS APIs are implemented across the breadth of the TMS320 family of DSPs. Any application built upon the DSP/BIOS kernel can be easily picked up and moved to a different TMS320 platform. The application code doesn't care that the underlying chip has changed because the DSP/BIOS provides a layer of hardware abstraction.

Scalability

The scalability of DSP/BIOS is like an *a la carte* menu at a restaurant. You pick exactly what you want and you get exactly what you want, and no more.

The concept of a Real-Time Operating System (RTOS) and kernels (the core pieces of an RTOS that handle basic resource management and thread scheduling) has been around for years. However, kernels and RTOS's are often bundled into large libraries that can't be easily scaled down when certain features are not required. The resulting problem is that code that is never going to be used gets linked into the final program and wastes valuable space. This type of issue isn't much of a problem in the microprocessor application where there's 32 MB of external memory, but it's an absolute killer in the DSP where that internal memory is so valuable.

DSP/BIOS solves this problem by being made up of a set of discrete modules that have reasonable independence from each other. That way, at program build time, only the required DSP/BIOS modules are linked in and all unused ones are left out. Some examples of the modules are things like:

- HWI (for hardware interrupt)
- SWI (for software interrupt)
- PIP (for pipe)
- PRD (for periodic function), and so on

The Integrated Development Environment, Code Composer Studio, includes a really cool graphical configuration tool. This tool, the DSP/BIOS configuration tool, lets you pick and configure DSP/BIOS modules as if you were reading an *a la carte* menu. Automatic program generation can then take place to assemble the required kernel modules and prepare them for linking into the application.

Design-time object creation

Memory is so precious on a DSP that TI opts to play some additional tricks to reduce the kernel footprint on the device. The technique relies heavily on the fact that the host-programming platform, usually a PC running Code Composer Studio, has all kinds of memory that the DSP doesn't. It's really a very asymmetric scenario. Why not use this asymmetry to your advantage?

TI does this by using the concept of *static module configuration*. Many DSP applications are quite static. By this, we mean that once the DSP has started running, its operational characteristics change very little, if at all. Many or most of the kernel objects simply need to be created once and then left to run for the life of the DSP (or until someone pulls the plug or battery). However, module creation consumes significant program and data space — that's valuable memory that you're trying to save.

An alternative approach is to use the resources of the *development host* (the PC running CCS) to perform the module creation once and leave the pre-created kernel modules to be linked into the application. This approach not only saves valuable memory, but because it's done at design time and not at run time, it doesn't have to be anywhere near real time.

Cases will crop up where the application calls for a module to be created at run time. DSP/BIOS supports this paradigm as well, but like all other kernels, it carries the additional baggage that allows this run-time creation.

Using Software Interrupts — A Lightweight Scheduling Mechanism

We discuss some of the advantages of using DSP/BIOS in terms of scalability, robustness, and portability in the previous section. But which pieces of the BIOS should you consider using to get the job done?

If your system is anything other than a simple one-algorithm, one-channel system, chances are you're going to need some kind of scheduler. Virtually every application needs some kind of scheduling paradigm to dish out CPU resources in a predictable fashion that ensures the system maintains real time.

In order for the DSP to maintain "real" real time, it sometimes must be able to pass the CPU from one activity (thread) to another thread before returning to the original thread.

Consider again our earlier metaphor of domestic bliss and the problem of scheduling the one bathroom among the five inhabitants of the "luxury" condo. Imagine that someone is in the bathroom shaving with the door locked, while someone else needs to quickly get in to use the toilet. The person needing to use the toilet clearly has a greater need than the person shaving, so perhaps the person shaving must leave the bathroom for a minute, allow the toilet user in, and then reclaim the bathroom a minute later. DSP scheduling works in much the same way — "shaving person" and "toilet-using person" are just like threads.

A common paradigm for such scheduling is to use a task model (DSP/BIOS TSK). However, these TSK modules are often overkill for many DSP applications. They are quite hungry in terms of both program size and data size because each task in the program requires its own *stack* (a section of memory dedicated to a thread for temporary storage of data). A lightweight version of a task is known as a *Software Interrupt* (DSP/BIOS SWI). Software Interrupts can achieve most of what a task can do but with a few limitations.

SWIs have priorities associated with them. You can assign various algorithms and processes different priorities in order to guarantee real real-time operation: a high priority SWI can interrupt a lower priority SWI. The only caveat is that the higher priority SWI must finish all of its work before giving the CPU back to the lower priority SWI. This process is known as "run to completion." The high priority SWI can still be interrupted by an even higher priority SWI, but then that one must finish before control is passed back down to the lower priority SWIs.

The reason that this approach is attractive is that all the SWIs in the system can share a single common stack. This turns out to give big savings in data memory. The actual code required to implement the SWI module is also simpler than that of TSK. So, if at all possible, it's a good idea to architect your system using SWIs. In Chapter 4, we put together some pre-built frameworks, one of which makes heavy use of the SWI concept. In Part II of the book, we show you how to build an entire application based on these concepts.

Figure 2-1 shows an execution graph from within Code Composer Studio. This example shows how various SWIs are being used to schedule out activities on the DSP. You can see higher priority SWIs taking over the CPU, and then when done, relinquishing it to the lower priority SWIs.

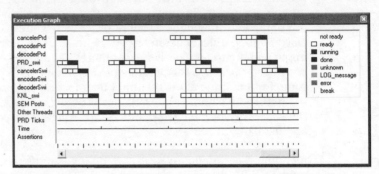

Figure 2-1: DSP/BIOS execution graph showing some SWIs in action.

Figure 2-1 also shows periods of time when no critical activity is running and the processor would otherwise be idle. However, you can do some useful stuff during this supposed idle time, as we discuss in the next section.

Real-Time Analysis

OK, time for a reality check.

You've just written your application and downloaded it to the target DSP, and it doesn't work as planned. What do you do? You would probably start by setting some breakpoints in the code, stopping the program, and then looking at registers and memory dumps for clues to the problem. You may find the problem, in which case you'll change some code, rebuild the program, download it, and try again.

But what if the problem doesn't show up? Or, what if the bug only shows up when the system is running at full speed and mysteriously disappears when you throw in breakpoints and other debug statements? This type of problem occurs all the time.

Thankfully, DSP/BIOS offers some real advantages in this area. Each of the BIOS modules is pre-instrumented in a way that useful data can be extracted from the system during run time. How is this possible?

As we mention in the previous section, there are periods of time in which the processor is really idle, that is, it isn't doing anything directly related to running the application. During this idle time, the processor can move useful data from the *target board* (that is, the board with the DSP on it) up to the *development host* (the PC running Code Composer Studio). This can be achieved via whatever connection (for example, serial cable, PCI bus, or USB cable) ties the host development platform to the target during the debug phase. The power and virtually unlimited memory of the development host can be used to take run-time debug data from the instrumented DSP/BIOS modules and display them in useful and easy-to-comprehend formats. For a good example, refer to the execution graph in Figure 2-1. All of this data is gathered for "free" — that is, at no cost to real-time performance of the DSP.

You, the user, don't have to do any additional programming. You just simply select to display the execution graph from the tools menu in the Code Composer Studio. The same is true for the CPU "load" graph and the statistics windows that show things like the number of times a module is executing and the average- and worst-case execution times. All of these real-time facilities are a boon to debugging a complex system.

Best of all, none of this instrumented code has to change from the version being debugged to the version that you ship. This really helps for two reasons. First, you have only one version of the code to maintain. Second, in the event of a problem in the field, the same real-time debugging facilities are available should they be needed.

Just How Big?

If all of these DSP/BIOS features sound useful, then you're probably asking yourself just how much footprint do these modules consume? This question has no single answer due to the scalability of the kernel and different DSP platforms like

TMS320C5000 and TMS320C6000. Table 2-1 shows some typical size numbers for the kernel in various configurations. Notice how, in a minimal configuration, the kernel can be as small as 1 kiloword (KW) on the C5000 DSP platform. That is truly small, leaving much of that precious internal memory for the rest of the application. That's what DSP programming is all about.

Table 2-1: DSP/BIOS Kernel Sizes for Different Configurations

Kernel Configuration	5402 (in 16 bit words)		6211 (in 8 bit bytes)	
	Code	Data	Code	Data
3 Software Interrupts, Interrupt Vector Table.	1040	158	5940	532
4 Software Interrupts, 1 Periodic Function, 2 Pipes, Real-Time Analysis, RTDX, Real-time Clock, Interrupt Vector Table	3178	897	14812	3132
4 Tasks, 2 Software Interrupts, 1 Mailbox, 1 Semaphore, 2 Pipes, Real-time Analysis, RTDX, Real-time Clock, Interrupt Vector Table	5519	1242	24024	4393

Chapter 3

Using XDAIS — Like Driving on the Same Side of the Road

● ●

In This Chapter

▶ Getting familiar with the DSP rules of the road

▶ Making use of code portability and flexibility

▶ Running multiple DSP channels with re-entrancy

▶ Sticking to the DSP naming conventions

▶ Sharing precious resources

▶ Relying on true performance measures for algorithms

● ●

*I*magine a world in which nobody agrees on which side of the road to drive. Then toss out speed limits — let's just have everyone go as fast as they want. Overtaking anywhere is perfectly permissible and by all means, do U-turns in the school zone. It's also fine if your car leaks oil onto the road, has bald tires, and belches blue clouds from the exhaust. Lastly, those seat-belts are just for decoration — you don't actually need to wear them.

Does all of this sound ridiculous? Most of these issues led to laws for reasons of safety, sharing the road, and the environment. We all grumble about many of them from time to time, but without many of these rules and guidelines, the roads really would become dangerous and chaotic. They're bad enough as it is!

The same is true for DSP software. In Chapter 1, we discuss why programming a DSP is somewhat different from programming a general purpose microprocessor. One of the key reasons (think really busy road) is the sharing of precious resources like internal memory, math execution units, specialized peripherals, and so on. Unless you have some rules and guidelines for sharing the DSP resources, chaos is likely to arise.

In DSP programming, lawlessness can manifest itself as a software algorithm making greedy and selfish assumptions about the assignment of precious resources all to itself and not sharing the "road" with other algorithms that also need to utilize the system resources. As a result, getting a useful working system when using the rogue algorithm would be difficult or impossible to do.

XDAIS (pronounced "Dayus" — the X is silent) is essentially the rules of the road for DSP algorithms that run on the TMS320 DSP platforms. There are rules that are mandatory and guidelines that are highly recommended but that can be violated if necessary. In the DSP world, the system integrator is really the person who benefits from or requires adherence to XDAIS. System integrators are the folks who have the very difficult job of taking code from disparate groups and even outside vendors and stitching it all together into a working whole. Knowing that all of the algorithms follow the XDAIS rules and guidelines is really beneficial. Even more helpful is that many algorithms have been officially tested for compliance to XDAIS and if and when they pass, they're allowed to declare that they are eXpressDSP compliant and show the mark in Figure 3-1.

XDAIS breaks down into four distinct areas, as we cover in the following sections.

Figure 3-1: The eXpress DSP Compliant logo.

Using Common Sense — Portability and Flexibility

Wouldn't it be great if every time a significant piece of DSP code like an algorithm is written, the code would be portable to other members of the DSP platform? And wouldn't it be useful if, without changing a single bit of code, the same algorithm code could be utilized in both simple and complex systems? Your answer is most likely yes to both of these questions. Portability and flexibility sound like just plain common sense. But some coding rules need to be followed to make this a possibility. Following these types of rules provides a level of portability and flexibility that system integrators will really appreciate.

Code re-locatability

All eXpressDSP-compliant algorithms need to be fully re-locatable. This means that they must not assume hard-coded addressing for both their own code and any data structures or buffers that they may depend upon. Doing so enables the system integrator to locate the algorithm code and data in the most desirable memory space, taking into account all other considerations of the system.

No direct peripheral access

Though a great temptation lies in having a key algorithm bang away directly on a key hardware peripheral, this situation creates disaster. The problem is twofold. First, other algorithms won't know when the peripheral is available. Second, the algorithm loses portability to another TMS320 DSP, which may have the same or similar peripheral but with different registers in different locations. To be eXpressDSP compliant, an algorithm must not directly access peripherals.

However, some algorithms require the use of Direct Memory Access Controllers (DMA) and practically speaking, need to interface directly to these controllers. To cope with this requirement, XDAIS supports a special DMA interface to meet this need. We touch on this more a little later in this chapter.

Re-entrancy

One of the beauties of modern DSPs is that they can run several simultaneous channels of the same algorithm. For example, suppose you have a DSP running 10 channels of voice coding. Having 10 copies of the algorithm code on the DSP would be very silly. A better way to operate is to have just one copy of the algorithm servicing multiple channels in some kind of scheduled fashion. However, servicing multiple channels in this manner can only be achieved if the algorithm is fully *re-entrant*. Re-entrancy allows an algorithm to be interrupted anywhere in its execution, save state for that channel, switch to another channel, run that new channel, then later come back to the original channel, restore state, and continue running.

A classic pitfall is the sloppy use of read/write global variables. If an algorithm uses a global variable, then there is a chance that the variable will be corrupted by the interruption and the operation of the original channel will be incorrect.

Static memory management

As mentioned previously, ideally any algorithm should be usable in a very compact software design all the way up to a very complex system. One of the common tricks in DSP programming is to use so-called *static resource allocation*. You are probably familiar with dynamic resource management with concepts like run-time memory allocation using a function like `malloc()`. The `malloc()` function certainly is useful, but it has certain serious limitations in compact DSP software systems. First of all, `malloc()` requires actual code space to run. Second, `malloc()` takes precious time to run. And third, `malloc()` can take a variable amount of time to run — not good where real real-time is so important.

Wouldn't it be useful if the required memory buffers could be statically created before actual run-time and then `malloc()` could be avoided altogether? Well, here's the good news: eXpressDSP supports exactly this notion of static resource allocation. What's even better is that all XDAIS algorithms can be used in either their native dynamic mode or run in a static mode. All of this without changing a single line of code in the algorithm itself. That is true portability!

Let's All Be Consistent

A second group of rules in the XDAIS algorithm standard mandate a level of consistency from all TMS320 DSP algorithms. In the car analogy, this group of rules equates to having everyone drive on the same side of the road. While the decision to pick right or left is somewhat arbitrary, having everyone agree to do the same thing in a particular country really helps.

Register usage

Each DSP in a family has multiple registers for program usage. Some are general purpose and several are for peripheral control. In particular, the DSP/BIOS (discussed in Chapter 2) makes use of certain bits of registers for its own correct operation.

Now imagine integrating an algorithm into a system also using DSP/BIOS, but not knowing which register bits are hands-off. The result can be one of those annoying bugs that shows up infrequently and is extremely tricky to track down. The solution is to have a list of registers (or bits of registers) that algorithms must not use and get everyone to agree to that list. This is another function of XDAIS. Each TMS320 DSP platform has a clear list of which registers can or cannot be used.

Naming conventions

Lots of good (and several bad) naming conventions are in common use. All of the good ones have merits (that's what makes them good), but they're also all different.

Given that the DSP/BIOS kernel is in use in almost all TMS320 DSP designs anyway, XDAIS mandates the usage of the DSP/BIOS naming conventions. Arbitrary? Perhaps. But as with driving on the same side of the road, better arbitrary and consistent than inconsistent.

Endianess

As we mention earlier, the decision of which side of the road is the "correct" side (we won't say the *right* side) is arbitrary.

Regardless, the decision is necessary. When it comes to 32-bit microprocessors, the decision is whether to go big or little.

32-bit microprocessors have the inherent characteristic of having two different ways to arrange the data within the 32-bit (4 byte) word, also known as *endianess*. Do you put the most significant byte at the lowest or highest address in memory? Does anyone care? It's somewhat arbitrary until you try and mix and match software that has been written with different endianess assumptions. For example, the TMS320C6000 platform of DSPs supports both little-endian and big-endian formats. XDAIS mandates that all algorithms be supplied in at least little-endian format. Providing the big-endian format is recommended, though not required. What is *not* OK is to supply a big-endian version only.

Perhaps you're wondering what a lot of these "rules" have to do with you. If you are simply going to be a user of prewritten algorithms, then the answer is not that much. A good analogy here is the electrical code. When you buy an electrical appliance, say a toaster, you simply plug it in and it works. You don't need (or want to read) the electrical code to get good toast. However, if you're manufacturing toasters, then you probably need to be quite familiar with the electrical code in order to produce a safe and reliable product. The same applies to XDAIS. If you really need to know the gory details, refer to the TI technical document SPRU352 — "TMS320 DSP Algorithm Standard Rules and Guidelines."

Sharing the Precious Resources

In Chapter 1, we spent quite a bit of time discussing the precious resources that a DSP has and how programmers need to manage those resources carefully to get the best overall results. XDAIS does its part to make this task easier. Special interfaces have been defined to enable this capability. One mandatory interface for all algorithms is known as IALG interface (short for the Instance Algorithm Interface).

The IALG interface

The IALG interface deals directly with the memory management for algorithms in the system. One thing XDAIS prohibits is the allocation of memory directly by an algorithm itself. Why is this? Well, left to supervise themselves, most algorithms would selfishly grab as much precious internal memory as possible in order to achieve best performance.

The problem occurs when that algorithm is integrated with other algorithms and now needs to share the "road" with these other algorithms. The solution to this problem is to not have algorithms assign memory at all. Instead, XDAIS mandates that the controlling framework or application assign memory on behalf of algorithms. This feature of XDAIS is made possible through the query/response mechanism of the IALG interface.

Essentially, the controlling framework queries all the algorithms in the system as to their memory requirements. This query includes the number of buffers, size of the buffers, type of memory, and memory alignment. Once the framework has queried all of the algorithms, it can then make smart decisions about who gets what. Even though algorithm A requests all of the precious internal memory, the system integrator may have determined that it's better to give that memory to algorithm B and provide slower memory to algorithm A. This decision of the system integrator may lead to better overall system performance because the system integrator is the only person who can really determine the optimal system configuration.

Consider a real world example of a personal MP3 player with fingerprint authentication that allows access to the player controls. It's OK for the fingerprint recognition algorithm (algorithm A) to take a little longer (say 1.5 seconds instead of 1 second) so that the MP3 decoder (algorithm B) can maintain real real-time in the worst case decode scenario.

Figure 3-2 shows the flow that is followed for the interrogation of algorithms for required memory buffers and the subsequent issuance of appropriate memory buffers. The IALG interface is the core of the process.

IDMA2

For those algorithms that want to leverage the on-chip DMA controllers, there is another mandatory interface called IDMA2. This interface operates in a similar way to the IALG interface for memory, but is designed for the uniqueness of DMA controllers.

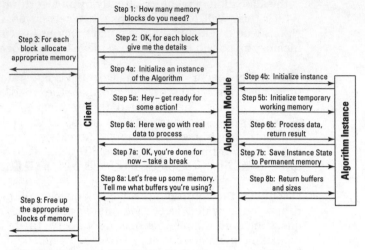

Figure 3-2: Diagram of IALG memory interface transactions.

Measurability

XDAIS mandates that all algorithms report critical performance numbers in a consistent fashion. This mandate allows better "apples to apples" comparisons. Some examples of these metrics include providing worst-case execution time, worst-case interrupt latency, and worst-case heap usage.

In summary, XDAIS and eXpressDSP compliance are the primary driving forces behind standardizing the look and feel of all algorithms designed to operate on the TMS320 DSP platforms. If you're going to build any kind of application on TMS320 DSP platforms, then you should strongly consider making eXpressDSP compliance a requirement. You'll thank yourself once you reach either the system integration phase or a later version of the product. More than 100 unique suppliers provide literally hundreds of different algorithms that comply to the standard. Some of the technology areas covered by this wide array of offerings include audio, video, telephony, voice, speech, biometric, communications, encryption, and many more. You can find the latest listing by going to www.dspvillage.com and selecting 3rd Party Network.

Chapter 4

Living in the Semi-Custom House — Reference Frameworks for the TMS320 DSP

. . . .

In This Chapter

▶ Understanding the benefits of standardized Reference Frameworks

▶ Trading size and performance with flexibility

▶ Getting to know the three levels of Reference Frameworks

. . . .

*W*e pretty much used up the automobile analogies in the last chapter, so it's time to think of something else that you interact with nearly everyday: your house or apartment, and we promise not to mention the bathroom and toilets anymore.

Take a moment to think about how modern-day houses go together. Depending on the type of house or apartment you live in, you have varying degrees of custom construction and reasonable price. The more custom work you get, the more you're going to have to pay for the final product.

Choosing an Architecture

Housing really has three basic categories: "full custom," "tract home," and the middle ground, "semi-custom." Choosing among these three types involves considerations of cost and, of course, how soon you can move into your home.

Choosing among your DSP programming options breaks out in much the same way, as the following sections explain.

Going full custom

The most expensive and unique houses are what one would describe as the "full custom home." In this scenario, you hire an architect to design your dream house. You spend lots of time on details to get things just right. The end result is often a beautiful home, but often with some serious drawbacks. First and foremost is time — a lot of calendar time is taken up from conception to completion.

The DSP programming version of this scenario is the fully custom DSP application. You, the programmer, decide to build the application from scratch. You decide to use nothing off the shelf, just pure custom code for your application. You have total control over everything, the source code is all yours, and you know exactly how to debug it. But there are serious downsides also. Completing this project is going to take the longest time and it's going to be expensive. You may miss a critical market opportunity due to the project schedule. Are you sure that you're really adding value in all of that code? Are there pieces of code that are really commodity status? Does the full custom approach really give you the extra differentiation to justify all the extra effort?

"Just add water" — the off-the-shelf solution

Let's go to the other extreme. In the housing world, this extreme is typified by the apartment or so-called "tract home" approach to construction. All the homes are basically identical with perhaps the exception of the paint scheme and the landscaping. The good news with this approach is speed. These homes get built very quickly because they are so similar. The builders literally learn the pattern once and then proceed to churn them out. Doing so keeps their cost and your cost low. However, this approach has obvious downsides as well. The biggest disadvantage is a lack of differentiation, that is, your home looks identical to that of your neighbors, and your neighbors' neighbors.

The DSP programming version of this scenario is the case where you buy a complete off-the-shelf software package to run on the DSP. An off-the-shelf solution provides for extremely quick time to market, but clearly severely limits the opportunities for differentiation. In fact, your competitor down the street can probably buy exactly the same off-the-shelf software solution and come to market with an almost identical product. The choice in the marketplace may come down simply to price, and you probably don't want to end up there.

Semi-custom — the best of both worlds

Wouldn't it be great if there was a middle ground? Well, in the construction business, there is, and it's called the "semi-custom home." Instead of hiring an expensive architect, you can buy a set of plans (often referred to as blueprints) for a number of styles of homes that have proven out by previous builders/customers for a reasonably low cost. The good news is that it's fairly easy to customize the house as you go along. You can pick all of the kitchen appliances, the plumbing fixtures, the lighting fixtures, the door styles, the flooring material, and so on. You can even change the configuration of some of the rooms, perhaps leave out a wall to open the kitchen into the living area, or even reverse a couple of rooms. You could alter the roofline, the roofing material, the gutters, and even add or subtract skylights. You get the idea. Even better is that you might find a builder who has actually built one of the plans and knows the ins and outs of the particular design. Doing so will also help to speed up construction and lower costs.

In the TMS320 DSP world, the semi-custom design is the eXpressDSP Reference Framework. Think of it as that blueprint for your software application. eXpressDSP provides a great starting point for your application. You have plenty of room for customization, but lots of the dirty work of the basic design has already been developed and tested. This semi-custom design approach gives you the best of both worlds — you can customize and differentiate, but you also keep your total development cost and time to completion way down.

Leveraging the Existing Infrastructure

In the building world, the semi-custom home is not only pre-designed, but it also heavily leverages existing infrastructure and standards. The foundation is probably assumed to be brick or concrete. When was the last time you saw a new home being built on sand or gravel? No point reinventing the wheel here — simply order in the cement mixers.

Likewise with the electrical system, which is most likely 120V or 220/240V throughout the house. This system is great because all of those appliances and gadgets you're about to go out and buy will simply plug in and work. A multitude of other standards and foundational elements can be found inside houses that really make the whole process efficient.

The eXpressDSP Reference Frameworks work much the same way. They strongly leverage DSP/BIOS (think bricks and cement foundations) and also XDAIS (think electrical code and plumbing codes). This information makes it much easier to architect a variety of designs without having to consider, discuss, or argue the foundation and standards for that design. Instead you can focus on questions like "What kind of home are you looking for?" A cottage, a two-story, five-bedroom home, or a mansion?

Different Levels of Reference Framework

Think about the semi-custom house-design approach. The basic questions you need to answer before picking a design are things like: do you want a single- or two-story home? How many bedrooms do you want? How many bathrooms? (Oh well, we mentioned bathrooms again). Do you want a separate dining room? How about a wine cellar?! You can see how these sorts of basic questions quickly lead you to a fairly limited set of blue-print choices. And even within those choices, some common themes in the construction techniques are going to crop up.

Exactly the same philosophy applies to eXpressDSP Reference Frameworks. Many applications can be grouped into a limited number of categories. TI refers to these categories as different levels of Reference Frameworks.

These Frameworks provide the ultimate answer to how to get going with your application development. They eliminate that nasty "staring at the blank sheet of paper" feeling. They help to get you started as well as help you to transition into your final application. They are available in C-source code form so that you can take complete control of the code for further adaptation and long-term maintenance.

Three Reference Frameworks currently are available: RF1, RF3, and RF5. Think of RF1 as the one-bedroom, one-bathroom cottage. Think of RF5 as the mansion with multiple bedrooms and bathrooms. RF3 provides a good middle ground between RF1 and RF5. Table 4-1 shows the Reference Frameworks selection matrix, which details some of the basic differences among the three.

Table 4-1: Reference Frameworks Selection Matrix

Design Parameter	Compact – RF1	Flexible – RF3	Extensive – RF5
Absolute minimum footprint	Yes	No	No
Static configuration	Yes	Yes	Yes
Static memory management	Yes	Yes	Yes
Single-rate operation	Yes	Yes	Yes
Number of channels	1-3	1-10+	1-100+
Number of eXpressDSP algorithms	1-3	1-10+	1-100+
Dynamic memory allocation	No	Yes	Yes
Multi-rate operation	No	Yes	Yes
Implements control functionality	No	Yes	Yes
Thread preemption	No	Yes	Yes
Blocking	No	No	Yes
Total memory footprint	3.5 KW	11KW	28KW
Part Number	RF1	RF3	RF5

In DSP application terms, take a look at the factors that affect the choice of the appropriate Reference Framework. In the simplest terms, the simpler the application, the more likely that RF1 or RF3 is the suitable starting point. For the more complicated application, choosing RF3 or RF5 is more appropriate.

The Compact Framework — RF1

Again, think of the one-bedroom, one-bathroom cottage. Key issues in the design are small size, simple materials, little or no flexibility, and low cost. The Compact Framework (RF1) achieves these goals for small and resource-constrained applications. Examples of these types of applications might include a speakerphone, smart toy, or digital headset. These systems demand an absolute minimum footprint from the framework so that space is left for application specific algorithms. The complete application must often fit in a very compact 8KW or 16KW internal memory. The need for external memory is often a deal-killer in these types of applications, either due to cost, power, or physical space.

The design of RF1 makes certain assumptions and thus enables the construction of a modular, structured framework for the application. By far the most important assumption is that the system is comprised of a small number of channels and algorithms that will be run. In fact, the range of 1 to 3 is appropriate for both of these parameters. The system objects must be statically configured, meaning that no support exists for run-time object creation (kiss those expensive create functions good-bye!). It also assumes that memory is managed statically, avoiding run-time memory allocation. This type of configuration is usually quite acceptable for simple applications where the functionality is fixed and not likely to change for an extended period of time.

The design also assumes that all the algorithms in the system run at the same data rate and that data is synchronously passed from one algorithm to the next. This assumption provides additional simplification to the framework, further reducing the overall footprint.

Finally, even though the framework supports XDAIS algorithms, another trick is played to further reduce overhead. Algorithms are queried statically to get requirements before the application is ever run. That way, the run-time overhead of buffer management can be eliminated.

Finally, RF1 assumes that no other processor exists within the system. This eliminates the need to support a communication thread between the DSP and any other processor. The end result of all the above assumptions is a complete eXpressDSP Reference Framework implemented in less than 4KW.

The Extensive Framework — RF5

Now that you have a feel for the one-bedroom, one-bathroom cottage, take a look at the other extreme — the multi-bedroom, multi-bathroom mansion. Anyone who builds a mansion is most likely not so concerned with limited space and to an even lesser extent, cost. Most likely, the important criteria are lots of rooms, different types of rooms, flexibility, configurations, and modularity.

The same is true in the DSP application space. RF5 is designed for systems where the numbers of channels and algorithms can range from a handful to literally hundreds. For true flexibility, this framework supports the use of DSP/BIOS TSKs (tasks) for thread management. This method of thread management enables one channel/algorithm to be completely blocked and/or suspended by a higher priority TSK in the system. Such an arrangement is very useful in complex systems where the system designer is doing everything possible to maintain real-time operation.

This design also enables multi-rate operation, meaning that different channels/algorithms can be run at different data and frame rates and yet the framework can stay on top of everything. You can also choose whether to use static or run-time memory management. The choice of static helps with the overall framework size, but choosing dynamic memory management allows the ultimate run-time flexibility.

Finally, a separate thread is made available for communication to another system processor such as a general-purpose processor. This other processor can establish a messaging scheme between itself and the DSP utilizing this dedicated DSP thread.

Of course, all of this flexibility comes at a price in terms of footprint. Reference Framework 5 uses about 28 KW of memory. But just like the designer of the mansion, this larger footprint is secondary to the flexibility that the framework offers.

The Flexible Framework — RF3

Happily, a middle ground exists between the one-bedroom cottage and the mansion. In the case of Reference Frameworks, it's the Flexible Framework — RF3.

RF3 is a good compromise between the two other current frameworks, RF1 and RF5. RF3 is designed for a multitude of systems with simple to mid-range complexity. TI recommends the use of RF3 for systems with 1 to 10 channels of operation and 1 to 10 algorithms in the system. These limits are not hard and fast, but simply recommended guidelines.

RF3 assumes static configuration, but does allow dynamic memory management techniques. It is built on the DSP/BIOS SWI (software interrupt) paradigm for thread scheduling. As explained in Chapter 2, SWIs allow thread pre-emption, but not blocking the same way TSKs (tasks) do. This means that the highest priority SWI will always run to completion before the next lower SWI can run. This prioritization has significant implications in terms of memory-usage savings due to reduced stack usage and smaller, simpler scheduling objects.

RF3, like RF5, does support multi-rate operation and also provides a dedicated thread for external interface/control. This additional flexibility over RF1 comes at a small price in terms of framework memory footprint. RF3 consumes about 11KW on a TMS320C54x processor.

An example of an application requiring an absolute minimal, but still structured framework, is a digital hearing aid, as shown in Figure 4-1. The user wants the batteries to last dozens of hours at a time and the entire application, including the required sound processing algorithms, needs to fit entirely in the internal memory of the low cost DSP. By not having any external program memory, physical size is reduced, power consumption is lowered, and cost is kept to a minimum. RF1 serves the purpose ideally.

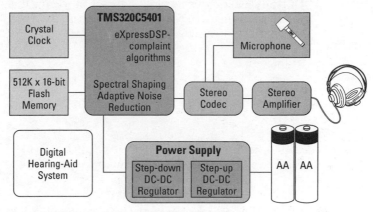

Figure 4-1: A hearing-aid application using RF1.

Part II of this book shows you how to build a real working audio recording/playback device starting with the Flexible Framework RF3. The power of the Reference Framework becomes clear when you see how quickly you can have your application up and running, how easily you make changes, and how simple it is to switch in and out different versions of the core algorithms. Only when building an application can you truly see the power of the well-architected, robust, pre-written software for TMS320 DSPs.

Part II
Building a Real Application Today

The 5th Wave   By Rich Tennant

"Yes, it's wireless, and yes, it weighs less than a pound, and yes, it has multiuser functionality... but it's a stapler."

In this part . . .

OK, it's time to roll up your sleeves and build a real application.

Have you ever wondered how those digital music players work? Well, in this part, we take you through an example of setting up a low-cost development board and then actually constructing a software program that runs an audio recorder/player. By the time you're done, you'll have music flowing through your application.

Chapter 5

Introducing the DSP Starter Kit and Tutorial

● ●

In This Chapter

▶ Providing for real-time audio

▶ Understanding the underlying signal processing

▶ Avoiding "blank page" syndrome

▶ Building your applications with a blueprint in place

● ●

*A*fter reading Part I, we hope that you are curious enough to put some of what we say to the test. What better way to do this than to build a simple DSP application and see for yourself how easy it is?

In this chapter, we introduce you to the DSP Starter Kit (DSK). The DSK includes the software and hardware to quickly and easily build custom DSP applications to fit your needs.

Getting Started with the Audio Player/Recorder Project

As a way of demonstrating the DSK, we've developed a tutorial that takes you through the steps of building a simple audio player/recorder using the DSK as the hardware platform. An audio player/recorder is a good model for demonstrating DSP applications because, though easy to build, it makes use of many of the fundamental capabilities of a DSP.

The play/record capability needs to use an algorithm to compress/decompress the data so that it doesn't take up too much memory on the DSP. The system also needs "play through" capability, meaning that the system needs to be able to take real-time audio input and output it to a speaker, even while it is being recorded. After all, getting data into and out of the system is a major component of DSP system design.

Figure 5-1 shows a schematic of the audio player/recorder.

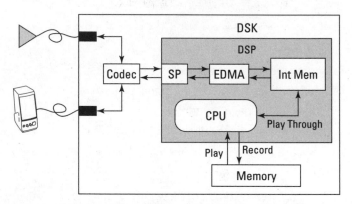

Figure 5-1: The audio player/recorder system.

Considering System Needs

Before digging into the instructions for building the audio player/recorder in Chapters 6 and 7, take a minute to consider what this system will need.

Input and Output (I/O)

An obvious need is the ability to get the data into and out of the system. This process is accomplished with a device driver that initializes and controls the audio codec on the DSK and the peripherals connecting it to the DSP (I/O read/write).

Device drivers are where "the rubber meets the road" in a DSP system, or at least where the software meets the hardware. Device drivers allow system architects to build applications that are independent of the hardware on which the application will run. This feature allows designers to quickly move applications from one hardware platform to another.

Processing

After the audio data has been acquired, what do you do with it? In an audio player/recorder with play-through capability, you have two essential functions to perform:

- **Play-through.** For this mode, the application will require code to copy acquired buffers from input to output so that audio captured at the input can be sent to the output for play through a speaker.

- **Record and playback.** For this mode, the application requires algorithms to compress and store the audio (record) and decompress the audio (playback). A simple Storage module will be used to store the encoded data and retrieve the decoded data from DSP memory.

User control

The system needs to offer the user a way to choose which mode to use: play-through or play/record.

Getting Past the Dreaded Blank Page

OK, now that you know what you need, you're just about ready to get started.

If you were to open Code Composer Studio, TI's integrated development environment, and start a new project, you would probably see something like what you see in Figure 5-2:

Figure 5-2: The dreaded blank-page syndrome.

Who wants to start this way? What painter loves to stare at a blank canvas? What writer looks forward to writer's block? Who says developing DSP systems is any different? Is it any less creative to sit down and write code on a page rather than poetry? No way!

The good news is that you don't have to start this way.

Starting smoothly with Reference Frameworks

In the construction world, blueprints make it possible to build the same home over and over again. They also make a good starting place for building a similar home with some modifications.

What if you had a software application "blueprint" that was already built so that you could use it as a starting place for your application? A blueprint that

 ✔ Does something useful.

 ✔ Is easy to adapt and change to suit your needs.

 ✔ Defines modules that can be reused.

✔ Includes documentation and comments.

✔ Is written in portable, high-level language.

✔ Has a well standardized file structure.

✔ Uses various development tools together.

✔ Is NOT a blank page.

Reference Frameworks from Texas Instruments are these blue-prints. They are part of the eXpressDSP Software and are provided as starterware for developing applications that use DSP/BIOS and the TMS320 DSP Algorithm Standard (also known as XDAIS).

The Reference Frameworks provide starting points for your applications. They are flexible and written with the idea that someone (like you) is going to come along and try to adapt them to fit specific needs.

Going forward with the tutorial

You will be using Reference Framework Level 3 (RF3) for your audio player/recorder application. RF3 is intended to enable designers to create applications that use multiple channels and algorithms while minimizing the memory requirements by using static configuration only (see Part I for more explanation).

The key design goal for RF3 is ease-of-use. RF3 is architected to enable new DSP designers to create compact products with several algorithms and channels. RF3 provides more flexibility than lower Reference Framework levels. For example, RF3 instantiates any XDAIS algorithm simply and efficiently.

However, RF3 is not intended for use in large-scale DSP systems with 10s of algorithms and channels. Rather, RF3 targets medium-complexity systems and makes design decisions such as using static configuration to keep the memory footprint small.

Chapter 6

Starting with the Reference Frameworks

*I*t's finally time to start getting down to business. As we introduced in Part I and discussed further in Chapter 5, the Reference Frameworks provide a beginning to your DSP application — a blueprint that can be customized to meet your specific needs while being built on a solid and well-documented foundation.

The basic process to building an application using the Reference Frameworks goes like this: You first select the Reference Framework Level that best approximates your system and its future needs. You can then adapt the framework and populate it with eXpressDSP-compliant algorithms. Because common elements such as memory management, device drivers, and channel encapsulation are pre-configured in the frameworks, you can focus on your system's unique needs and achieve better overall productivity. You can then build on top of the framework, confident that the underlying pieces are robust and appropriate for the characteristics of your target application.

Because the Reference Framework Level 3 (RF3) provides a good balance between speed and ease of application development and flexibility, we use RF3 in the audio player/recorder tutorial.

Getting to Know the Basic Reference Framework Level 3

By default, the RF3 application, as shown in Figure 6-1, converts an incoming audio signal to digital data at a given sampling rate. It splits this signal into two signed 16-bit samples, one for the left and one for the right channel. (For a stereo codec, the signal is split. For a mono codec, two channels are emulated by duplicating each mono sample to the left and right channels.) The application then processes both channels independently by applying a low-pass filter to the left channel and a high-pass filter to the right channel. It then applies a volume control to each channel. Finally, the two channels are merged into one before being sent to the output. The volume for each channel can be selected at run time.

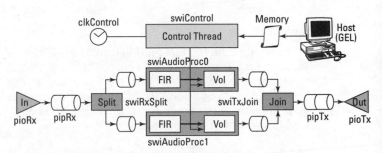

Figure 6-1: The RF3 default application.

The default application behavior simply provides an example of the behavior of applications suited to using RF3. The application logic can easily be modified while leaving the data flow path in place.

Installing and Running the RF3 Application

This section describes how to build and run Reference Framework Level 3 (RF3) as it is. Later sections describe how the application works and how it can be adapted for your audio player/recorder application.

The following sets of numbered steps are general steps. For more specific instructions related to hardware or software installation, take a look at the documentation provided with your DSK.

Preparing the hardware

The board-specific portions of the RF3 application have been ported to several boards. The following steps provide an overview of how to connect the hardware to your host PC. For details and diagrams, see the documentation provided with your board.

1. **Shut down and power off your PC.**

2. **Connect the appropriate data connection cable to the DSK board.**

3. **Connect the other end of the data connection cable to the appropriate port on your PC.**

4. **Connect an audio input device, such as a microphone or the headphone output of a CD player, to the audio input jack (or jacks) on the DSK board.**

   You can also connect the audio output of your PC sound card to the audio input of the board.

5. **Connect a speaker (or speakers) or other audio output device(s) to the audio output port(s) of the DSK board.**

6. **Plug the power cable into the DSK board.**

7. **Plug the other end of the power cable into a power outlet.**

8. **Start the PC.**

Preparing the software

The following numbered steps outline the software installation and setup steps required to run RF3. For details, see the appropriate Quick Start Guides, online help, or the readme.txt file.

1. **If you haven't already done so, install CCStudio 2.2 or a later version.**

   We recommend that you have the latest version of the CCStudio software, as it may contain important features or problem fixes.

2. **Check the configuration of your parallel printer (LPT) port (if applicable).**

   If your board supports a parallel emulation interface, then make sure the parallel port is in ECP or EPP mode and note the first address of the port. This is normally 0x378. For details on checking the parallel port configuration, see the Quick Start Guide provided with your board.

3. **Use the Setup Code Composer Studio application to configure the software for your board.**

   For details, see the documentation provided with your board.

4. **Download the Reference Frameworks code distribution for this application from** www.ti.com/dummiesbook.

5. **Place this file in any location and unzip the file.**

   The myprojects\ folder under the folder where you installed CCStudio is a suggested location for these files.

   The top-level folder of the Reference Frameworks distribution is called referenceframeworks. The full path to this folder is called RF_DIR in the remainder of this chapter.

Building and running the RF3 application

After installing the package, you are ready to build and run the RF3 application.

1. **Within CCStudio, click Project⊅Open and select the** app.pjt **project in** RF_DIR\apps\rf3\target **where** *target* **matches your board. (For example,** RF_DIR\apps\rf3\dsk6x11.**)**

2. **Click Project⇨Build to build the RF3 application.**

3. **Click File⇨Load Program and load the** app.out **file in the Debug subfolder.**

   Be patient, as loading the executable into DSP memory takes time.

4. **Start your CD player or other audio input.**

5. **Click Debug⇨Run (or press F5).**

   You should hear the FIR filtered audio output through the speakers connected to the target board.

6. **Click File⇨Load GEL and select the** app.gel **file from the project folder (above the Debug folder).**

   GEL or General Extension Language is an interpretive language that enables you to write functions to config-ure the Integrated Development Environment (IDE) and access the target processor. In this case, the app.gel file is a GEL script file that displays some graphical user interface (GUI) controls. When you move these controls, the script writes certain values to the target's memory. These values control which of the two channels is active and the volume level for each channel.

7. **Click GEL⇨Application Control⇨Set Active Channel.**

   A slider with two positions appears. The positions select the output channel. The down position selects channel 0, which uses a low-pass filter. The up posi-tion selects channel 1. Channel 1 uses a high-pass filter, which makes the music sound somewhat better.

8. **Click GEL⇨Application Control⇨Set_channel_0_gain.**

   A slider appears with values for channel 0's volume ranging from 0 to 200. The default value is 100. Channel 0 must be the active channel for the slider to produce audible changes.

9. **Similarly, to control the volume of channel 1, click GEL⇨Application Control⇨Set_channel_1_gain, and use the slider to control channel 1's volume.**

Looking Under the Hood: Exploring the RF3 Application

The following steps will help you familiarize yourself with how the RF3 application works behind the scenes:

1. **Start Code Composer Studio by double clicking on the CCS icon on the desktop.**

2. **Open the project called** app.pjt, **located in** RF_DIR\apps\rf3\target **(where *target* matches your board), by clicking Project⇨Open...**

3. **Use the project view window on the left side of the screen to examine this project.**

All of the header files included in the project are listed in the Include folder, and all of the .c files are located in the Source folder. You can open any of these files by navigating to the correct folder and double-clicking on the file that you are interested in.

The project file

The application project file, app.pjt, includes all the .c and .h files in the rf3\ folder, as well as app.cdb file and the link.cmd linker-command file.

Compilation information flow

The diagram in Figure 6-2 shows the flow of header files. An arrow in the diagram indicates that the file at which the arrow ends includes the file from which the arrow starts.

Global data objects

To aid understanding of the program execution flow, this section lists all non-DSP/BIOS global objects and functions in the RF3 application.

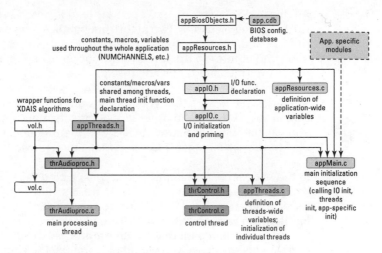

Figure 6-2: Flow of header file information.

To implement threads, you make a thread-specific data structure that encapsulates the thread's private state information for each thread. Some of the information in the structures is determined statically at load time, some is determined in initialization time, and some, of course, is used and modified throughout the life of the thread.

First, take a look at the Audioproc thread data structure:

```
typedef struct ThrAudioproc {
    /* algorithm(s) */
    FIR_Handle  algFIR;     /* an instance of the
FIR algorithm */
    VOL_Handle  algVOL;     /* an instance of the
VOL algorithm */

    /* input pipe(s) */
    PIP_Handle      pipIn;

    /* output pipe(s) */
    PIP_Handle      pipOut;

    /* intermediate buffer(s) */
    Sample          *bufInterm;

    /* everything else that is private for a
thread comes here */

} ThrAudioproc;
extern ThrAudioproc thrAudioproc[ NUMCHANNELS ];
```

As this code shows, an Audioproc thread is described with the following elements: two algorithm handles, one each for the FIR and VOL algorithms; one pointer to the thread's input pipe, one pointer to the thread's output pipe; and one pointer to the intermediate buffer the thread uses.

The principle here is that you do not want to "hardwire" the thread to DSP/BIOS and other global objects it uses. Rather, you use handles for all the objects and then "connect" handles to the actual objects in the initialization phase.

In the Audioproc0 example, you statically bind the pipIn handle to the pipRx0 pipe, and the thread's run() function never refers to pipRx0 but always to pipIn when reading input. If you were to put another thread before the Audioproc0 thread in the data path that would preprocess the block Audioproc0 receives, you would only modify the connection in the static initialization without having to change the thread's run-time code.

The same applies for the output pipe and the address of the intermediate buffer the thread uses.

All global objects used in the RF3 application are shown in Figure 6-3, which depicts the final RF3 application's data path.

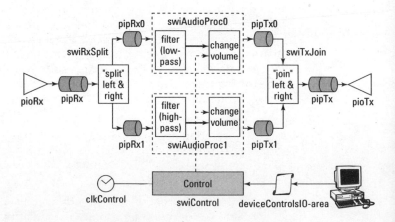

Figure 6-3: RF3 Application Data Path and Global Objects.

Source code files

This section briefly explains the purpose and content of important source files in the application. For detailed information, see the actual files, which are well commented.

- ✔ appBiosObjects.h: This file "exports" all the DSP/BIOS objects to which the application code may refer, including PIP objects and LOG objects. Since this file is at the root of the inclusion tree, those objects are visible to every module.

- ✔ appResources.h: This file contains application-wide macros, data types, and function/data declarations that may be used throughout the application. It is similar to appBiosObjects.h files, except that appBiosObjects.h contains information about DSP/BIOS objects only.

- ✔ appResources.c: This file should *define* (that is, allocate space and initialize, if needed) all the global variables declared in appResources.h. RF3 doesn't have any such variables (except for the UTL_sts objects, which are used for real-time analysis), so this file is essentially empty.

- ✔ appIO.h: The appIO.h file declares two I/O functions — appIOInit() and appIOPrime() — for initializing I/O devices and for *priming* I/O pipes. Priming refers to placing initial zero frames in the pipes. Priming must be a separate operation from initializing, since I/O devices are usually initialized first and primed as the last operation in the main() calling sequence. This place is where you should define the interface to any other application-specific functions your application needs, if you have them.

- ✔ appThreads.h: Analogous to appResources.h, which defines information needed throughout the entire application, appThreads.h defines macros and constants, and declares variables and functions that are needed by the threads in the system.

- ✔ appMain.c: This file contains the application's main() function. It includes the global resource header file, appResources.h, and the header files defining the interface to I/O and the threads, appIO.h and appThreads.h. The main() function calls appIOInit(), `appThreadInit()`, and `appIOPrime()`. It then exits and gives control to DSP/BIOS. In your application, this file should perform any other necessary initialization.

✔ `appIO.c`: The `appIO.c` file is the core location for board-specific code. A different version is provided in the folder for each board. This file encapsulates calls that differ due to varying codecs and sample rates. It implements the I/O initialization and priming, and it defines the two `PIO` objects.

✔ `fir.h, fir.c, vol.h, vol.h`: These four files provide function wrappers for the two dummy XDAIS algorithms provided. They let the application call algorithm functions in a "friendly" way. For example, the application can call the `FIR_apply(<params>)` instead of using the `firHandle->fxns->filter(<params>)` syntax. These function wrappers increase the readability of the application code.

✔ `ifir.c, ivol.c`: Files `ifir.c` and `ivol.c` contain default algorithm instance parameters and are provided by the vendor. We simply copied these files into their local folders and included them in the application. It is recommended not to modify these files, but to overload the parameter values at initialization time.

✔ `thrAudioproc.h`: The `thrAudioproc.h` header file defines the `Audioproc` thread's data structure and external interface. Here is the structure again:

```
typedef struct ThrAudioproc {
    /* algorithm(s) */
    FIR_Handle  algFIR;      /* an instance
of the FIR algorithm */
    VOL_Handle  algVOL;      /* an instance
of the VOL algorithm */
    /* input pipe(s) */
    PIP_Handle      pipIn;
    /* output pipe(s) */
    PIP_Handle      pipOut;
    /* intermediate buffer(s) */
    Sample          *bufInterm;
```

```
     /* everything else that is private for
a thread comes here */

} ThrAudioproc;

extern ThrAudioproc thrAudioproc[ NUMCHAN-
NELS ];
```

An Audioproc thread has a FIR handle for a FIR
instance, a VOL handle for a VOL instance, a PIP handle
for an input pipe, a PIP handle for an output pipe, and a
pointer to an intermediate buffer. Anything else that
encapsulates the state of the thread would be placed
here as well.

By grouping private data this way, you can create arrays
of threads, which you indeed do: one Audioproc thread
for each channel. When a thread runs, the thread knows
its index — channel number — which it uses to access its
data structure.

Other than the standard declaration of the thread's
init() and run() functions, this thread has the following declarations as well:

```
extern IFIR_Fxns FIR_IFIR;      /* FIR
algorithm */

extern IVOL_Fxns VOL_IVOL;      /* VOL
algorithm */
```

As you know, an eXpressDSP compliant algorithm is iden-
tified by its function table. For the FIR algorithm, the
function table is of type IFIR_Fxns and is named
FIR_TI_IFIR. At the linking stage, you define the
vendor-independent FIR_IFIR symbol to be equal to
FIR_TI_IFIR. This enables you to use a different
vendor's FIR algorithm without recompiling the application, and instead, just by relinking it.

✔ thrAudioproc.c: This file is the core of the application,
as it implements the thread that processes the data
streams by calling XDAIS algorithms. As with other
threads, it has three parts:

  • **Static initialization of the thread's data object.**
    Static initialization is similar to that of other

threads. You declare the thread object(s) and "connect" the pointers to actual objects in the data path. For Audioproc, it is one input pipe, one output pipe, and one intermediate buffer. Since NUMCHANNELS is 2, you initialize that many Audioproc threads in an array. Ideally, you try to initialize statically as much as possible. However, with the ALGRF module, the XDAIS algorithm instances must be created dynamically, so you use NULL for their initial values.

- **Run-time initialization of the thread.** The next phase is dynamic initialization. The code first prepares static parameters that are used in the dynamic initialization. In the default case, you have two sets of FIR filter coefficients, one for a low-pass filer and one for a high-pass filter. Your algorithms may require other static data that you can initialize this way.

  The thrAudioprocInit() function must initialize *all* instances of the Audioproc threads, in this case thrAudioproc[0] and thrAudioproc[1]. For each thread in a loop, it creates and initializes all XDAIS algorithm instances the thread uses.

  For each thread, you first create one FIR instance and one VOL instance, thus initializing the algFIR and algVOL fields in the thread's data structure. You create a FIR instance by assigning the default parameters structure to a local parameters variable and then changing the fields that differ from the defaults. You do this similarly for the VOL instances.

- **The run() function called by the SWI object.** The thrAudioprocRun() function is fairly straightforward. The function is called by the swiAudioproc0 and swiAudioproc1 objects, which pass 0 and 1 as the argument, respectively. The chan argument is the channel number, which is used to access the correct thread data structure.

  The function follows the regular pattern of getting the input and allocating the output pipe, determines the addresses and sizes of both frames, processes the input frame, and stores the result in the output frame after calling FIR and VOL. The input for FIR is the input frame and the output for

FIR is the intermediate buffer. The intermediate buffer is the input for VOL, and its output is the output frame. Finally, it frees the input pipe and submits the output pipe before it exits.

✔ thrControl.h, thrControl.c: The control thread is a PRD thread. Part of the control process is the thrControlIsr() function as well, which is called by the clkControl CLK object every tick. The latter simulates a regular interrupt routine that is called when an external control-related hardware event occurs. This ISR reads the pretend-I/O registers containing the current value of two sliders (volume for each channel) and one switch (selection of active channel). These "I/O registers" in the deviceControlsIOArea integer array are really written by the GEL script or the debugger in the watch window.

✔ appThreads.c: The purpose of appThreads.c is to define all the global variables used across all threads — the intermediate buffer Sample bufAudioproc[FRAMELEN] in this case — and to implement the thrInit() function that initializes all threads.

✔ link.cmd: The linker command file link.cmd governs the linking process. As its first step, it includes the automatically generated appcfg.cmd file, which places different sections of the executable in their appropriate memory regions, as defined in the MEM section of DSP/BIOS configuration. The appcfg.cmd file also generates various other DSP/BIOS linking information.

In this application, the link.cmd file includes all the libraries the application uses: the device controller libraries and the libraries for the PIO, UTL, ALGRF, FIR_TI, and VOL_TI modules and algorithms. It also assigns the vendor-dependent algorithm function table symbols to generic function table symbols.

✔ app.gel: This GEL source file is very simple. It displays three sliders, one that ranges only from 0 to 1 with step 1 and is used as a selector between the two channels, and two volume sliders, one for each channel. Every time the user moves a slider, appropriate GEL procedures are called and they write the new values in the target's deviceControlsIOArea array. When writing, CCStudio temporarily halts the target and stores the value, and then resumes. This pause causes slight disruption in the output sound.

Using GEL scripts to simulate control is a simple and effective way to test the application in the early stages of development.

Chapter 7

Building the Audio Player/Recorder

● ●

In This Chapter

▶ Removing what you don't need from the Reference Framework application

▶ Adding the player and recorder threads

▶ Incorporating the encoder and decoder processing engines

▶ Building, running, and monitoring the application

● ●

*I*n this chapter, we discuss the adaptation of the RF3 application and show you how to build and implement the Audio Player/Recorder shown in Figure 7-7, which appears later. To build the Audio Player/Recorder, you first create audio encoder (recorder) and decoder (player) threads consistent with other threads in the system. Then, you integrate and schedule the two threads into the system. Finally, you populate the two threads with their respective G.723 Encoder or Decoder XDAIS compliant algorithm to support the record (compression) and playback (decompression) functions respectively.

The G.723 is an algorithm for compressing speech at 5.3/6.3 kbps, thereby providing a compression ratio of more than 20:1. Both algorithms ship with Code Composer Studio (CCS) as de-tuned algorithm examples to use for testing.

The G.723 algorithms used in this example are provided only for certain boards. If they are not available for your platform, adapt the steps as necessary to integrate the eXpressDSP-compliant algorithms you plan to use in your application.

Removing the Second Channel

Figure 7-1 shows a block diagram of the general RF3 application out of the box.

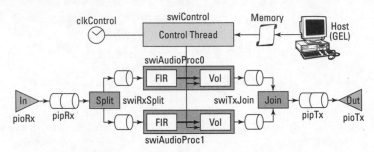

Figure 7-1: A block diagram of the RF3 application.

A lot of capability is built into this little application. It provides a good level of flexibility with minimum system impact. The functional breakdown of the RF3 application can be summarized as follows:

- ✔ **IOM drivers for audio codec input and output.** IOM, or I/O Mini-Driver Interface, is a simple, low-level device driver interface between application threads and block-oriented hardware devices.

- ✔ **Two processing threads with Filter and Volume algorithms for processing left and right channels.** The application processes each channel by applying a filter to the data. The left (first) channel data is applied to a low-pass filter, and the right (second) channel data is applied to a high-pass filter. A volume control is then applied independently to each channel, both channels having possibly different amplification/attenuation factors.

- ✔ **Split/Join threads to move data to and from processing threads.**

- ✔ **Control thread to support user channel and volume selection inputs.**

However, RF3 has a lot of stuff that you don't need for the single channel player/recorder application we show you how to build in this chapter. For example, the application only requires one channel between the codec input and output, and it doesn't require filtering. You can remove these capabilities from the RF3 application by following these general steps:

1. **Remove the Split and Join threads and the second channel.**

2. **Replace the Finite Impulse Response (FIR) algorithm with a VOLume control for the line output.**

3. **Modify the Control thread to support the second VOLume control.**

We don't cover the specific steps for removing the second channel here and instead focus on integrating the codec. Take a look at the SPRA793 application note for the steps to remove the second channel. SPRA793 is available in the Reference Frameworks area of the DSPvillage website (http://www.dspvillage.com).

Figure 7-2 shows a block diagram for the resulting single channel RF3 application that will be the starting point for the audio player/recorder application.

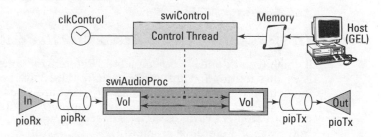

Figure 7-2: The single-channel RF3 application.

Adding Play and Record Threads

In this section, we show you how to create two threads: One for the *encoder* (recorder) and one for the *decoder* (player).

The first step is to add the encoder and decoder threads into the system, as shown in Figure 7-3.

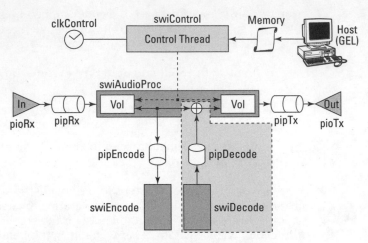

Figure 7-3: The encoder and decoder threads.

The integration is such that the gain-adjusted audio from the line input can be recorded simply by enabling the encoder. The output from the decoder (player) is mixed with the gain-controlled audio coming into the system at the line input. This mixed audio signal is then routed to the line output, where it can be connected to a speaker or headphones for listening.

Inspecting the encoder thread

If you haven't done so, download the Reference Frameworks code distribution for this application from www.ti.com/dummiesbook.

Note: Customers with CCS DSK licenses, check out "eXpressDSP Reference Frameworks Release Notes" at www.ti.com\ dummiesbook for details on updating and rebuilding your CCS projects.

1. **Open the project called** app.pjt **located in** RF_DIR\apps\xdsp_part1*target*, **where** *target* **matches your board, by using the Project⇨Open... menu command.**

   A Code Composer Studio project stores file-and-build information for a particular application.

2. **In the CCS Project View window, open the Include, Source, and DSP/BIOS Config folders.**

   These folders list all header and source files included in the application.

Getting familiar with the encoder thread data structure

In this part, we show you how the encoder thread is added to the system.

1. **Open the header file** thrEncode.h **by double-clicking the file in the Project View window.**

   This header file defines the ThrEncode thread data structure and external interface. The following code shows the structure of this thread:

   ```
   typedef struct ThrEncode {
       /* active? */
       Bool enabled;

       /* output pipe */
       PIP_Handle pipEncode;

       /* everything else that is private for
   a thread comes here */
       Sample *bufIntermediate;

   } ThrEncode;
   ```

   A ThrEncode thread has a "Record" on/off status Boolean variable called enabled; a PIP handle for an input pipe from the audio processing thread (see pipEncode in Figure 7-3); and a pointer to an intermediate buffer for processing. The thread also has the standard declarations thrEncodeInit() and thrEncodeRun().

2. **Open the source code file** thrEncode.c **by double-clicking the file in the Project View window.**

   Similar to the implementation of the audio processing thread in Chapter 6 in thrAudioproc.c, the encoder thread also consists of the same three parts:

   - **Static initialization of the thread's data object.**
     In this case, the encoder is disabled by default. The element pipEncode points to a statically declared pipe module, &pipEncode, which can be found in the .cdb file. The last element in the data structure is bufIntermediate which points to the bufAudioproc shared with the other thread.

```
ThrEncode thrEncode = {
    /* active */
    FALSE,

    /* output pipe(s) */
    &pipEncode,                      /* pipEncode
*/

    /* intermediate buffer */
    bufAudioproc,                    /*
*bufIntermediate */
}
```

- **Run-time initialization of the thread.** The thrEncodeInit() function is intentionally left empty here because the encoder thread won't be doing any encode processing. We go into more detail on this function again later when we discuss integrating encoding functionality using a XDAIS algorithm in the section, "Creating, initializing, and running an algorithm instance using ALGRF."

- **The run() function called by an SWI object.** The thrEncodeRun() function is fairly straightforward and represents the execution sequence for encoding/recording audio stream coming from the thrAudioproc thread. This execution sequence is:

1. **Verify that a full audio buffer is available in pipEncode from thrAudioproc thread.**

```
UTL_assert( PIP_getReaderNumFrames(
thrEncode.pipEncode ) > 0 );
```

The UTL_assert( ) function is part of the UTL module that comes with RF3. The UTL module has functions to observe the program on the DSP (the target). The UTL_assert( ) function tests a condition to see if it is true or false. In the example above, PIP_getReaderNumFrames( ) returns the number of frames available to the reader. If this happens to be 0, then there has been an error in the application and it doesn't continue executing.

2. Get a pointer to data frame from the
pipEncode.

```
PIP_get( thrEncode.pipEncode );
```

3. Encode/Record if enabled.

We address this part of the run() function in
later sections. For now, no encoding is done
regardless of the enable state.

4. Return empty buffer to pipEncode data pipe.

```
PIP_free( thrEncode.pipEncode );
```

 The thrEncodeRun() function is called by the swiEncode
object, which we cover in the section, "Creating, initializing,
and running an algorithm instance using ALGRF" later in this
chapter.

Initializing the encoder thread

The encoder thread still needs to be initialized by the application every time the system starts executing. The following
steps introduce this process:

1. **Open the source code file** appThreads.c **by double-**
clicking the file in the Project View window

2. **Inspect the encoder thread initialization in**
thrInit() **function.**

```
Void thrInit( Void ) {
    .
    .
    .
    thrAudioprocInit();    /* Audioproc thread */
    thrControlInit();      /* Control thread   */
    thrEncodeInit();       /* Encode thread */

}
```

3. **In the CCS Project View window, open the DSP/BIOS**
Config folder.

4. **Open the configuration file** app.cdb **by double-click-**
ing the file in the Project View window.

5. **In the Scheduling:SWI folder, click on** swiEncode
and inspect its properties.

Note that the `thrEncodeRun` function that is called every time the SWI is run.

6. **In the Input/Output:PIP folder in the .cdb file, click the pipe** `pipEncode` **and inspect its properties.**

Note that in this case, the reader of this pipe is the encoder thread `swiEncode`, which is posted using `SWI_post` every time a full buffer is available in the `pipEncode`.

Implementing the Decoder Thread

Now that you have seen the essential parts necessary to add a thread to a system, it's time to add the decoder thread. In this section, you need to write the code necessary to add the decoder to the system.

1. **Click Project⇨Add Files to Projects... and select the source code file located in** RF_DIR\ apps\ xdsp-part1\appModules\thrDecode.c.

Add this file to the project.

2. **Click Project⇨Scan All File Dependencies.**

This command parses all the source files and includes all needed header files in the Include folder.

3. **Open the header file** thrDecode.h **by double-clicking the file in the Project View window.**

4. **Modify the** ThrDecode **thread data structure to define:**

   • A boolean variable called `enabled`.

   • A handle to a pipe object called `pipDecode`.

   • A buffer pointer called `bufIntermediate` of type Sample.

This modification is similar to `ThrEncode` defined in `thrEncode.h`.

5. **Click File⇨Save to save the file.**

6. **Click File⇨Close to close the header file** thrDecode.h.

7. **Open the source code file** thrDecode.c.

8. **Setup** `thrDecode` **structure declaration with the following default values:**

   - `FALSE`. Active state disabled.

   - `&pipDecode`. Address of pipe connecting the decoder thread to the audio processing thread.

   - `bufAudioproc`. Address of intermediate buffer shared between all threads.

   Again, this is similar to the initialization of the `thrEncode` in `thrEncode.c`.

9. **Modify** `thrDecodeRun()` **to:**

   - Allocate pipe buffer from pipDecode using `PIP_alloc()` and `PIP_getWriterAddr()` functions.

   ```
   PIP_alloc( thrDecode.pipDecode );
   dst = PIP_getWriterAddr(
   thrDecode.pipDecode );
   ```

   Use the comments that are provided in the file to help you decide where to put this code.

   - Record amount of actual data being sent out using `PIP_setWriterSize()` function.

   ```
   PIP_setWriterSize( thrDecode.pipDecode,
   sizeInWords( FRAMELEN ) );
   ```

   The above statement is one line of code.

   - Put data buffer in pipe using `PIP_put()` function.

   ```
   PIP_put ( thrDecode.pipDecode );
   ```

   Note how `thrDecodeRun()` is returning a zero-filled buffer using `memset()` when the decoder is disabled.

10. **Save and close the source file** `thrDecode.c`.

That's it — you've completed the implementation of the decoder thread. However, the decoder thread still needs to be initialized by the application every time the system is turned on.

Initializing the decoder thread

1. Open the source code file `appThreads.c` by double-clicking the file in the Project View window.

2. Add the following code to `thrInit()` function:

```
thrDecodeInit();          /* Decode thread */
```

Make sure you include `thrDecode.h` at the top of the file in order to have access to `thrDecodeInit()` function.

3. Save and close the source code file `appThreads.c`.

Scheduling the decoder thread: Adding the SWI object

1. In the CCS Project View window, open the DSP/BIOS Config folder.

2. Open the configuration file `app.cdb`.

3. In the Scheduling:SWI folder, right-click SWI–Software Interrupt Manager and select Insert SWI.

4. Right-click the newly inserted SWI (`SWI0`), and select Rename.

5. Rename `SWI0` to `swiDecode`.

6. Right-click `swiDecode` and select Properties.

7. Set the properties for the SWI to call `_thrDecodeRun`.

Change only one property here. The default values for the others will be fine for now.

8. Click OK.

Adding the `PIP` object: Creating the data path from the decoder to the audio processing thread

1. In the Input/Output:PIP folder, right-click PIP–Buffered Pipe Manager and select Insert PIP. Rename newly inserted PIP to `pipDecode`.

2. Right-click `pipDecode` and select Properties.

3. Change the following properties of `pipDecode`:

General	Change to:	Notify Functions	Change to:
bufalign:	32	NotifyWriter:	_SWI_post
framesize(words):	120	nwarg0:	_swiDecode
numframes:	1	NotifyReader:	_SWI_andn
		nrarg0:	_swiAudioproc
		nrarg1:	8

Integrating the Decoder and Encoder Threads

Now you understand the encoder thread and you've added the decoder thread implementation. You also have pipDecode and pipEncode in place providing a data path between the threads. In this section, you connect this data path (the PIP modules) to the audio processing thread, thrAudioproc, and modify its implementation to process data across the new data path at the right time.

 All encoder related modifications are already implemented for simplification and for your reference when implementing the decoder side of the application.

Connecting pipEncode and pipDecode to the audio processing thread

1. **Open the header file** thrAudioproc.h.

   As depicted in Figure 7-3, the audio processing thread ThrAudioproc has the following interface:

   - line-input data pipe,
   - line-output data pipe,
   - encoder data pipe, and
   - and decoder data pipe.

2. **Modify the** ThrAudioproc **data structure to include a decoder data pipe and call it** pipDecode.

3. **Save and close the header file** thrAudioproc.h.

4. **Open the source file** thrAudioproc.c

5. **Include** thrDecode.h **to the beginning of the file.**

   Next, you need to initialize the audio thread data structure to connect it to the decoder data pipe.

6. **Modify the** thrAudioproc **static declaration to assign** &pipDecode **to the decoder pipe handle.**

   You can refer to thrAudioproc.h to determine the assignment location within the data structure.

Integrating the encoder and decoder thread data path in the audio processing thread

Before going further with the audio player/recorder, first take a look at the the thrAudioprocRun() function. Note the implementation of the encoder data path. Audio data is placed in pipEncode for processing by the encoder thread.

The following steps outline what's going on in thrAudioprocRun():

1. **First, you need to verify that a free frame buffer is available in** pipEncode **to write to.**

   ```
   UTL_assert(PIP_getWriterNumFrames(
   thrAudioproc.pipEncode ) > 0 );
   ```

2. **Next, allocate that frame buffer from the PIP and get a pointer to it.**

   ```
   PIP_alloc( thrAudioproc.pipEncode );
   dstEncode = PIP_getWriterAddr(
   thrAudioproc.pipEncode );
   ```

3. **Then you need to copy line-input audio mixed with decoded audio to the allocated buffer.**

```
for (i = 0; i < FRAMELEN; i++) {
    dstEncode[i] =
thrAudioproc.bufIntermediate[i];
}
```

4. **Then you need to put the frame buffer back in**
   pipEncode, **making it available to the encoder**
   thread.

```
PIP_put( thrAudioproc.pipEncode );
```

So, you need to mix the decoder data path (play-back audio)
with audio from the line-input. To do so, follow these steps:

1. **Insert the following code into the**
   thrAudioprocRun() function:

```
UTL_assert( PIP_getReaderNumFrames
    (thrAudioproc.pipDecode) > 0 );
PIP_get( thrAudioproc.pipDecode );
srcDecode = PIP_getReaderAddr(
thrAudioproc.pipDecode );
for (i = 0; i < FRAMELEN; i++)
{
    thrAudioproc.bufIntermediate[i] +=
srcDecode[i];
}
PIP_free( thrAudioproc.pipDecode );
```

2. **Save and close the source code file** thrAudioproc.c.

Rescheduling the audio
processing thread

So far, you've incorporated the encoder and decoder thread's
data path into the audio processing thread. Next, you need to
reschedule the audio processing thread to run when a decoded
audio frame is available in pipDecode and an empty frame is
available in pipEncode. Here's how:

1. **Open the configuration file** app.cdb, **if it is not**
   already open.

2. **In the Scheduling:SWI folder, right-click**
   swiAudioproc **and select Properties.**

3. Set the mailbox value to 15.

What this does is reserve two additional bits in the SWI mailbox to allow notification from the encoder and decoder threads. The resulting mailbox for swiAudioproc and notifying data pipes are depicted in Figure 7-4.

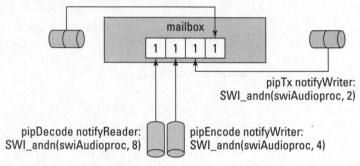

pipRx notifyReader:
SWI_andn(swiAudioproc, 1)

pipTx notifyWriter:
SWI_andn(swiAudioproc, 2)

pipDecode notifyReader:
SWI_andn(swiAudioproc, 8)

pipEncode notifyWriter:
SWI_andn(swiAudioproc, 4)

Figure 7-4: The swiAudioProc (mailbox).

4. Save and close the DSP/BIOS Configuration file app.cdb.

Building and running the Project

1. Click Project⇨Rebuild All to build the project.

2. Click File⇨Load Program and load the executable .\Debug\app.out.

3. Set up the audio input by starting the audio source on your computer.

4. Click Debug⇨Run from the Debug menu.

If everything is running correctly, you should hear the audio. If you don't, check to make sure everything is set up according to the "Preparing the Hardware" section in Chapter 6.

Viewing the Execution Graph

The Execution Graph shows the system you built in action. Pay special attention to the two new threads that you added to the system: the encoder and the decoder. To open the Execution Graph tool, **click DSP/BIOS⇨Execution Graph.** You should see something like Figure 7-5.

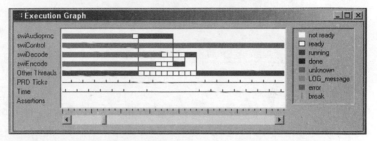

Figure 7-5: The Execution Graph in action.

Figure 7-5 shows a typical Execution Graph when the Audioproc thread runs. When it runs, it gives a buffer to the encoder and takes a buffer from the decoder. The way the application is set up, the encoder and decoder threads will run when these buffers are exchanged. These threads don't really do anything yet, but you can still make sure that they are running using the Execution Graph. Doing so verifies that you have the system set up properly before you move on. The signaling and setup must be correct or they won't run.

Viewing the CPU load

The CPU Load Graph gives an idea of how much load the system is under when an application is running.

To see the CPU Load Graph, **click DSP/BIOS⇨CPU Load Graph**.

You should see something like Figure 7-6.

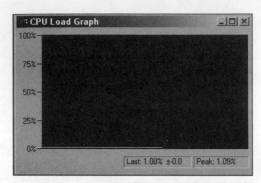

Figure 7-6: The CPU Load Graph.

Halting and resetting the system

When you are through checking out the Execution Graph and the CPU Load Graph, make sure to halt the DSP and Reset the system. Here's how:

1. **Click Debug⇨Halt to halt the CPU.**

2. **Click Debug⇨Reset CPU to reset the processor.**

3. **Click Project⇨Close.**

Remember to close your project prior to opening a new one. Otherwise, you may have multiple projects in your project window, which can be confusing.

Adding the Player and Recorder Engines

In this section, we show you how to:

✔ Populate encoder and decoder threads with XDAIS compliant voice encoder and decoder algorithms using the RF3 ALGRF framework module.

✔ Interface the encoder and decoder threads to a simple STORAGE module for recording and playback of encoded and decoded audio.

The resulting system diagram is shown in Figure 7-7.

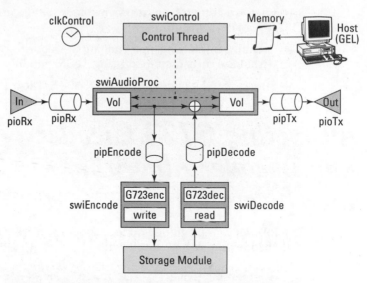

Figure 7-7: The integrated encoder and decoder algorithms.

The ALGRF module exists to create and delete XDAIS algorithms by using the DSP/BIOS MEM memory manager. It is a Reference Framework service that simplifies the use of XDAIS components in end applications. Any module that implements IALG (that is, any XDAIS compliant algorithm) can be used with ALGRF.

In this section, we show you how to use ALGRF to create, initialize, and run instances of the XDAIS compliant voice encoder and decoder algorithms as part of their respective threads. We also show you how to interface the encoder and decoder threads to a STORAGE module using the STORAGE_store and STORAGE_retrieve functions respectively. This simulates recording and playing of compressed audio to and from FLASH memory.

The integration described in Figure 7-7 is such that the playback audio from the decoder is mixed in with the gain-controlled audio coming into the system at the line input. The mixed audio signal is then routed to the line output for listening. The provided integration of the encoder algorithm into the encoder thread includes the following:

> ✔ Encapsulating the algorithm instance handle into the thread data structure.
>
> ✔ Creating, initializing, and running the algorithm instance within the thread context using ALGRF module.
>
> ✔ Interfacing the encoder output to the STORAGE module.

Inspecting G723 Encoder and Decoder Algorithm Interface Files

The following steps guide you to inspect the G723 encoder and decoder algorithm interface files:

1. **Open the project called** `app.pjt` **located in** `RF_DIR\apps\xdsp-part2\target`, **where** `target` **matches your board.**

2. **In the CCS Project View window, open the Include and Source folders.**

3. **Click Project⇨Add Files to Projects...**

   Add source code files `g723dec.c` and `ig723dec.c` from the `RF_DIR\apps\xdsp-part2\algG723DEC\` directory to the project.

   The interface files for the encoder algorithm are already included for you.

4. **Click Project⇨Scan All File Dependencies.**

   This parses all source files and includes all needed header files in the Include folder.

5. **Open the following source code and header files by double-clicking the file in the Project View window to inspect their content:**

   - `g723xxx.c`: This file contains concrete APIs that the ALGRF framework can use to interface to the algorithm. This file is not included as part of the XDAIS compliant library.

- g723xxx.h: This file defines the interface for the concrete APIs.

- ig723xxx.c: This file contains the default values for the creation parameters of each algorithm instance. It is used by ALGRF framework to obtain default values for the algorithm.

- ig723xxx.h: This file defines the module specific interface.

Inspecting G723 encoder algorithm integration

In this section, you examine the code that is necessary to add the encoder algorithm to the system. Then, we show how to add the decoder algorithm to the system.

Adding a handle to the algorithm instance to the thread data structure

Open the header file thrEncode.h. This header file defines the ThrEncode thread data structure and external interface. Here's the structure:

```
typedef struct ThrEncode {
    /* active? */
    Bool       enabled;

    /* algorithm(s) */
    G723ENC_Handle  algG723ENC;  /* an
instance of the G723ENC algo
          rithm */
    /* output pipe */
    PIP_Handle      pipEncode;

    /* everything else that is private for
a thread comes here */
    Sample         *bufIntermediate;

    /* compressed data storage in memory */
    STORAGE_Obj    storage;
} ThrEncode;
```

A ThrEncode thread has a "Record" on/off status Boolean variable, a handle to an encoder algorithm instance, a PIP handle for an input pipe from the audio processing thread (see pipEncode in Figure 7-7), a pointer to an intermediate buffer for processing, and a pointer to a storage object for recording encoded audio.

Creating, initializing, and running an algorithm instance using ALGRF

Open the source code file thrEncode.c. Similar to the implementation of the audio processing thread in thrAudioproc.c, the encoder thread also consists of three parts:

✔ **Static initialization of the thread's data object.** In this case, the encoder is disabled by default. The algG723ENC handle is set to NULL as it will be initialized at run-time. The pipEncode points to a statically declared pipe module, &pipEncode. bufIntermediate points to the bufAudioproc shared with other thread. And, storage handle set to NULL for run-time initialization.

Here's the code:

```
ThrEncode thrEncode = {
    /* active */
    FALSE,

    /* algorithm handle to be initialized
at runtime */
    NULL,                    /* algG723ENC */

    /* output pipe(s) */
    &pipEncode,              /* pipEncode */

    /* intermediate buffer */
    bufAudioproc,            /*
*bufIntermediate */

    /* STORAGE object to be initialized at
runtime */
    NULL,                    /* storage */
}
```

✔ **Run-time initialization of the thread.** The
thrEncodeInit() function is called to initialize the
thread data structure by creating and initializing an
encoder algorithm instance and a storage handle. The initialization sequence is as follows:

   **1. Set the encoder algorithm creation parameter
structure to default values supplied in
ig723enc.c.**

```
g723encParams = G723ENC_PARAMS;          /*
default parameters */
```

   **2. Use the ALGRF framework API to create an
instance of the encoder algorithm and confirm
successful creation and report memory con-
sumed by the instance in the DSP/BIOS
Message Log tool using the UTL support
functions.**

```
thrEncode.algG723ENC = G723ENC_create(
    &G723ENC_IG723ENC,
    &g723encParams );
UTL_assert( thrEncode.algG723ENC != NULL );
UTL_showAlgMem( thrEncode.algG723ENC );
```

   **3. Create and initialize a storage object to inter-
face between the encoder output and the STOR-
AGE module.**

```
STORAGE_new( &thrEncode.storage );
```

✔ **The run() function called by the SWI object.** The
thrEncodeRun() function is fairly straightforward and
represents the execution sequence for encoding/record-
ing audio stream coming from the theAudioproc thread.
This execution sequence is

   **1. Verify a full audio buffer is available in
pipEncode from thrAudioproc thread.**

```
UTL_assert( PIP_getReaderNumFrames(
thrEncode.pipEncode ) > 0 );
```

2. Get a pointer to data frame from the pipEncode.

```
PIP_get( thrEncode.pipEncode );
src = PIP_getReaderAddr( thrEncode.pipEncode );
```

3. If the encoder is enabled, then encode the input data and store the resulting compressed (encoded data) in a storage medium (memory) using the STORAGE_store() **function.**

```
G723ENC_apply( thrEncode.algG723ENC,
        (XDAS_Int16 *)src,
        (XDAS_Int8 *)thrEncode.bufIntermediate);
done = STORAGE_store(
        &thrEncode.storage,
        thrEncode.bufIntermediate,
        sizeInWords(COMPRESSED_FRAMELEN));
```

4. Return the empty buffer to the pipEncode **data pipe.**

```
PIP_free( thrEncode.pipEncode );
```

The thrEncodeRun() function is called by the swiEncode object.

Linking and binding the encoder algorithm

1. Open the header file thrEncode.h.

Note the declaration of the generic function table for the XDAIS encoder algorithm G723ENC_IG723ENC. This will be bound to the actual function table at link time by the link.cmd file.

```
extern IG723ENC_Fxns G723ENC_IG723ENC;          /*
G723ENC algorithm */
```

2. Open the link command file link.cmd **by double-clicking the file in the Project View Window.**

Note the inclusion of the G723 library and the binding process of the generic G723ENC symbol the Texas Instruments implementation of the G723 Encoder function table at the end of the file.

```
-l g723_ti.l62
_G723ENC_IG723ENC = _G723ENC_TI_IG723ENC;
```

Integrating the G723 decoder algorithm

Now that you have seen the code needed to add the encoder algorithm, it's time to actually write the code to add the decoder algorithm to the system.

Adding a decoder algorithm instance handle to the thread data structure

1. Open the header file thrDecode.h.

2. Include g723dec.h and storage.h to have access to decoder and storage module interfaces.

3. Modify the ThrDecode thread data structure to add the following definitions:

   • A G723DEC_Handle variable called algG723DEC.

   • A STORAGE_Obj variable called storage.

   This is similar to ThrEncode defined in theEncode.h.

4. Save and close the source header file thrDecode.h.

Creating, initializing, and running an algorithm instance using ALGRF

1. Open the source code file thrDecode.c.

2. Modify the thrDecode structure declaration to set the algG723DEC and storage to NULL.

3. Check structure definition in thrDecode.h for field declaration order.

4. Create and initialize a decoder algorithm instance handle, verify creation, and report memory usage.

   To do so, add the following code to thrDecodeInit() function:

```
thrDecode.algG723DEC = G723DEC_create(
        &G723DEC_IG723DEC,
        &g723decParams );
UTL_assert( thrDecode.algG723DEC != NULL );
UTL_showAlgMem( thrDecode.algG723DEC );
```

5. **Retrieve an encoded buffer from storage and decode it when the decoder is activated and hence in playback mode.**

To do so, add the following code to `thrDecodeRun()` function. Use the comments provided in the code to help you decide where to put each function call.

```
STORAGE_retrieve( &thrDecode.storage,
        thrDecode.bufIntermediate,
        sizeInWords( COMPRESSED_FRAMELEN ) );
G723DEC_apply( thrDecode.algG723DEC,
        (XDAS_Int8 *)thrDecode.bufIntermediate,
        (XDAS_Int16 *)dst );
```

Note how `thrDecodeRun()` is returning a zero-filled buffer using `memset()` when the decoder is disabled.

6. **Save and close the source header file** `thrDecode.c`.

Linking and binding the decoder algorithm

1. **Open the linker command file** `link.cmd` **by double-clicking the file in the Project View Window.**

2. **Assign** `G723DEC_TI_IG723DEC` **to** `G723DEC_IG723DEC`.

`G723DEC_IG723DEC` **is declared in** `thrDecode.h`.

3. **Save and close the link command file** `link.cmd`.

Building and Running the Project

You're almost ready to give the project a whirl. The following steps take you through building the project.

1. **Click Project⇨Rebuild All.**

2. **Click File⇨Load Program and load the executable** `.\Debug\app.out`.

3. **Set up the audio input by starting the audio source on your computer.**

4. **Click Debug⇨Run from the Debug menu.**

   If everything is running correctly, you should hear the audio. If you don't, check to make sure that everything is set up according to the "Preparing the Hardware" section in Chapter 6.

5. **Open the Execution Graph tool (click DSP/BIOS⇨ Execution Graph).**

6. **Open the CPU Load Graph (click DSP/BIOS⇨CPU Load Graph).**

Recording and playing back audio

In the next set of steps, you finally get to see all your work come to life as a living, breathing audio player/recorder.

1. **Open the source code file** `thrEncode.c`.

2. **Add the** `thrEncode` **data structure symbol to the watch window.**

   To do so, click on the `thrEncode` data structure symbol and then right-click and select Add to Watch Window in the pop-up menu.

   If the audio suddenly stops while expanding or modifying entries in the Watch Window, simply stop and reset the CPU, reload the program, and try again. This situation occurs due to the hardware codec halting with excessive breakpoints set by the Watch Window updates and will be fixed in future versions of CCS. A way to reduce the number of breakpoints is to stop the CPU by using Debug⇨Halt before modifying the Watch Window. You can restart the CPU after modification is done by using Debug⇨Run. A similar workaround also applies when moving the GEL sliders.

3. **While the system is running and audio is playing, start recording by setting** `thrEncode:enabled` **in the watch window to 1.**

   Note the increase in the amount of runtime for the encoder thread in the execution graph. You should see something like Figure 7-8 accounting for the encoder algorithm processing time. The processing time is also reflected in your CPU Load display represented by the first hump in Figure 7-10.

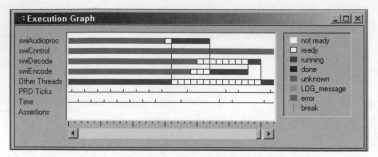

Figure 7-8: The Execution Graph with encoder processing module.

4. **Wait for about 30 seconds and then reset it to 0.**

   You have just recorded your compressed audio into external RAM.

5. **To play back the recorded audio, open the source code file** `thrDecode.c` **and add the** `thrDecode` **data structure symbol to the watch window.**

6. **While system is running, start playback by setting** `thrDecode:enabled` **in the watch window to 1.**

   You will hear a mix of recorded audio and current line-in audio.

If you hear pops and clicks, it's probably because the mix of the two signals is causing *clipping* (too much gain). You can try to minimize this by lowering your PC's output volume.

You can listen to playback audio only by setting the line input gain to 0. To do so, load the GEL file `.\app.gel` **(click File⇨Load GEL...)**. Then select Input_Volume from the GEL:Application Control CCS menu and set the slider to 0. All sliders initially are positioned at zero, even if the current value is not zero as is the case with the default line-input and line-output gains.

Note the increase in the amount of runtime for the decoder thread in the execution graph. You should see something like Figure 7-9 accounting for the decoder algorithm processing time. The processing time is also reflected in your CPU Load display represented by the second hump in Figure 7-10.

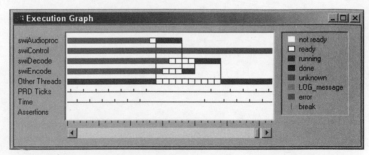

Figure 7-9: The Execution Graph with decoder processing module.

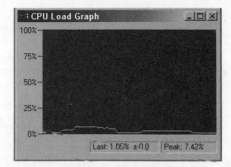

Figure 7-10: The CPU Load Graph with XDAIS modules.

Figure 7-10 shows the CPU load graph after enabling and disabling the encoder (the first hump) and then enabling and disabling the decoder (the second hump).

When you are through checking out all of this cool stuff, make sure to halt the DSP and Reset the system:

1. **Click Debug⇨Halt to stop the CPU.**

2. **Click Debug⇨Reset CPU to reset the processor.**

3. **Close the Project.**

Part III

The Part of Tens

The 5th Wave   By Rich Tennant

PCS Phones
- VOICE MEMO • VOICE MAIL
- TEXT MSG • CALL MGMT
- CONFERENCE CALL • FAX
- ALTERNATE LINE SERVICE
- CALLER ID • CALL FORWARD
- SIM CARD • SECURITY
- INTUITIVE MENU • H'
    "I" WAITING •
        • DATA TR.

"Do you have one with a longer antenna?"

In this part . . .

We include two chapters in the hallowed *For Dummies* Part of Tens. The first chapter tells you about a load of useful resources to further help you along with your eXpressDSP-based application, including useful technical documents and really cool Web sites. The second one reveals some really interesting trivia facts about eXpressDSP from its origin to its capabilities — enjoy!

Chapter 8

Ten Great eXpressDSP Resources

· ·

In this chapter

▶ Finding resources on the Web

▶ Building a kit of indispensable DSP tools

▶ Communicating with other DSP users

▶ Getting in-person training

· ·

*T*he following ten eXpressDSP resources are great places
to start if you want to go further with TMS320 DSP
programming. You can find everything from a simple tip from
a fellow DSP programmer to a full in-person training session.
The resources listed in this chapter also point you to the
hardware, software, and code to make your applications
come alive.

www.dspvillage.com

If you only remember one Web address, make it this one. This
Web site is *the* town square for programming a TMS320 DSP.
Everything else that you'll ever need can be found starting
from this point. The site has dedicated areas for software
where you can find tons of useful information on all of the
things we discuss in this book. Go to www.dspvillage.com
for more information.

www.dspestore.com

Here's a second address you need to know. This is the toy store of DSP development. Here you can buy DSP development tools, DSP development boards, emulators, software algorithms, and lots more. Check out www.dspestore.com for all the deals.

Code Composer Studio

If you need to write, develop, and debug a software program for a TMS320 DSP, then Code Composer Studio (CCS) is the development environment of choice. It's available in various forms. Initially, there are Free Evaluation Tools (see www. dspvillage.com above) that provide a 90-day evaluation period. A full version of the tools is available for $3595 (including maintenance). Check out www.dspestore.com for more details. Code Composer Studio is also included in the low-cost DSP Starter Kits (see the following section).

DSP Starter Kits

Need a fast and low-cost way to get started with TMS320 DSPs? Get yourself a DSP Starter Kit, or DSK as they're called. These kits start for as little as $295 and include a version of Code Composer Studio specifically for the development board. Part II of this book uses these popular development boards to show the power and flexibility of DSP.

Third-Party Catalog

More than 600 third-party vendors support the TMS320 platforms. These third parties range from algorithm vendors, emulator providers, and hardware board manufacturers. If you plan to purchase any algorithm code to run on a TMS320 DSP platform, we strongly recommend that you only purchase eXpressDSP compliant algorithms (see Figure 8-1). For more information on these providers and their products, check out www.dspvillage.com and select TI Third Party Products. Many third-party products are also available in the TI estore at. www.dspestore.com.

Figure 8-1: The eXpressDSP Compliant logo.

Signal-Processing Libraries

Sometimes, you just need basic signal-processing functions for your application. These functions are typically nuggets of code like a Finite Impulse Response (FIR) filter. Optimized versions of these code nuggets are provided in "libraries" of such functions. They are offered free of charge from TI. Visit www.dspvillage.com, select Software, and then choose Signal Processing Libraries.

Application Notes

Literally hundreds of application notes are available to help you get going or get finished with your TMS320 DSP design. Some of the application notes are generic and cover general subjects applicable to all designs, others are more application specific. They're all available from TI free of charge. They also often contain code snippets, which are great for copying into your application. Visit www.dspvillage.com, and under Technical Documents, select Application Notes.

Training

Sometimes, the best way to get up to speed on a product is to get some training. All kinds of training is available, ranging from 30-minute on-line overviews, all the way to 4-day in-person classes. Most of the on-line training is offered free of charge, whereas most of the in-person training classes require a payment. Check www.dspvillage.com, and under DSP Support, select Training & Webcasts.

Discussion Groups

Peer-to-peer discussion groups are a great way to ask questions and share experiences with the TMS320 DSP community. Discussion groups have been arranged by DSP platforms and also by application spaces. Participation does require registration, but is otherwise free of charge. Go to www.dspvillage.com, and under DSP Support, select Discussion Groups.

KnowledgeBase

If you have a question on signal-processing applications or any TMS320 platform, whether simple or extremely complicated, then try the KnowledgeBase server. Simply enter your natural language query (like, "How do I compile my code?") and see what comes back. The server is supported by a huge database and should produce very pertinent information and links to get you where you want to go. Visit www.dspvillage.com, and under DSP Support, select KnowledgeBase.

Chapter 9

Ten eXpressDSP Factoids

● ●

In This Chapter

▶ Finding new hardware

▶ Plugging in new capabilities for Code Composer Studio

▶ Testing your algorithms for XDAIS compliance

▶ Going further with your application development

● ●

*E*veryone loves trivia, so we included ten examples of our own in this chapter. However, this trivia is, in fact, not trivial — each of these features has a big impact on the success of your DSP applications.

Really Real Time

In any real real-time system, hardware interrupt latency must be as small as possible. With DSP/BIOS running on a 200MHz TMS320C6201, the interrupt latency is as little as *220 nanoseconds*. That's fast enough for virtually every conceivable application for such a DSP. Find more details in TI application note SPRA900.

System Visibility

As systems become more highly integrated, it's getting harder to see what's going on inside a running system. Emulation is great but often requires the target processor to be stopped to interrogate various registers and memory blocks.

Enter High Speed Real Time Data Exchange (RTDX) and the XDS560 emulator for use on TMS320 designs. With these products, it's possible to pass over *2 Mbytes/sec.* over the emulator cable, all the while running the DSP at full speed. That's fast enough to pass an MPEG video signal from the DSP to the development host for further analysis. Find more details at www.dspvillage.com.

Test Your Own Algorithms

Now you can test your own TMS320 DSP algorithms, for compliance with TI's TMS320 DSP Algorithm Standard, also known as XDAIS. Simply use the *QualiTI test tool* that comes bundled with the latest versions of XDAIS Developer's Kit, version 2.5 or later. The test takes just a few seconds to run. Download this Developers Kit from www.dspvillage.com.

eXpressDSP Reference Application Numbering Scheme

Here's some trivia for you. TI offers literally hundreds of application notes supporting development on the TMS320 DSPs. The numbering scheme for these application notes may appear cryptic — but look closer at the numbers for the eXpressDSP Reference Frameworks. For RF1, look at *SPRA791*, for RF3, look at *SPRA793* . . . get the pattern? So what's the application note number for RF5?

No April Fool 2002

April 1, 2002 represented the official launch date for the eXpressDSP Reference Frameworks. By the end of that year, more than 3000 different customers had downloaded the source code and more than 50 percent responded that they would be able to use some or all of the code. No joke! There must be some good stuff in there!

XDAIS Rules

Since eXpressDSP's introduction in 1999, the number of DSP algorithm programming rules has expanded to cope with new TMS320 devices, new types of algorithms, and new peripherals. The total number of rules now stands at 46. Refer to TI technical document SPRU352 for more details.

SPOX

No, it's not the latest disease making the rounds in Silicon Valley! SPOX was actually the first true kernel designed to run on the TMS320 DSPs in the early 1990's. SPOX was offered by a TI third party called Spectron Microsystems, based in Santa Barbara, California. TI acquired Spectron in the late 90s and from this came what is now known as DSP/BIOS. Many of the DSP/BIOS modules are based on code that has a 10+ year track record of robustness and proven operation in some of the harshest environments.

Boards Galore

We mention in this book that TI third parties offer hundreds of eXpressDSP compliant algorithms for your application. What is not such a well-known fact is that TI third parties also offer numerous types of development boards and tools. In fact, in the latest count, there are more than 400 different development boards, modules, and daughter cards available that all support the TMS320 DSP platforms. Check out www.dspvillage.com for that funky audio/video codec daughter-card that you've been looking for.

Virtual Team

The eXpressDSP team is truly a worldwide organization. There are teams in Houston, Texas; Santa Barbara, California; Toronto, Canada; and Bangalore, India. Imagine the fun involved in organizing teleconferences over all those time zones!

Code Composer Studio — Open?

Another not so well-known fact is that the Integrated Development Environment — Code Composer Studio — is open in such a way that many third parties are able to extend its capabilities through a plug-in approach. Many key industry players have taken advantage of this and offer cool plug-ins to further enhance your development experience. Check out www.dspvillage.com for more than two dozen of these plug-ins.

Index

• X •